THE

THRIFTY GUIDE TO

ANCIENT GREECE

A HANDBOOK FOR TIME TRAVELERS

THE THRIFTY GUIDE TO ANCIENT GREECE

A HANDBOOK FOR TIME TRAVELERS

Jonathan W. Stokes
illustrated by Xavier Bonet

VIKING

VIKING
An imprint of Penguin Random House LLC
375 Hudson Street
New York, New York 10014

First published in the United States of America by Viking,
an imprint of Penguin Random House LLC, 2018

Text copyright © 2018 by Tracy Street Productions, Inc.
Illustrations copyright © 2018 by Xavier Bonet Plaza

LIBRARY OF CONGRESS CATALOGING-IN-PUBLICATION DATA IS AVAILABLE
ISBN 9780451480279

Manufactured in China
Book design, maps, and graphs by Mariam Quraishi

1 3 5 7 9 10 8 6 4 2

For my family

PREFACE

The Thrifty Guide to Ancient Greece: A Handbook for Time Travelers was published holographically by Time Corp in the year 2164. It offers a complete vacation package for tourists visiting ancient Greece. A careless time traveler accidentally lost a copy of this handy guidebook in our own era, along with guides to ancient Rome, the American Revolution, and even medieval times. A New York publishing house decided to republish these books in 2018, beating Time Corp to market by more than a century.

The Thrifty Guide to Ancient Greece provides useful information for the practical time traveler:

  • How can I find a decent tunic that won't break my bank account?

  • Where can I score cheap theater tickets in ancient Athens?

  • What do I do if I'm being attacked by an army of five million Persians?

The guide answers this buzzing swarm of questions with the flyswatter of information. There are nifty nuggets on how to attend the ancient Olympic Games, how to meet your favorite Greek philosopher, and how you can help the Spartans win the Battle of Thermopylae without ending up on the wrong end of a Persian arrow. So wrap up your cloak and strap on your sandals. What follows is the original *Thrifty Guide to Ancient Greece*, as it was discovered on a sidewalk outside Frank's Pizza in Manhattan in AD 2018. . . .

THE THRIFTY GUIDE TO ANCIENT GREECE
A HANDBOOK FOR TIME TRAVELERS*

TIME CORP!™ SERVING YESTERDAY, FOR A BETTER TOMORROW, TODAY.™

....

* The Spoiler Alert Laws of 2162 will be abolished in the year 2165. But you probably knew that. Oh, wait, you didn't know that? Oops, sorry.

TIME CORP!™ SERVING YESTERDAY, FOR A BETTER TOMORROW, TODAY.™

INTRODUCTION BY TIME CORP CEO AND CORPORATE OVERLORD,
FINN GREENQUILL

Congratulations on purchasing *The Thrifty Guide to Ancient Greece: A Handbook for Time Travelers*, the best book in existence! The ancient Greeks gave the world democracy, philosophy, and theater, but that's nothing. I, Finn Greenquill, gave the world this book.

The Thrifty Guide to Ancient Greece comes with a money-back guarantee: we can almost guarantee you'll want your money back. Ancient Greece is filled with savage pirates, brutal mercenaries, and constant warfare. If this sounds like too much for you, you may want to purchase *The Thrifty Guide to Not Being a Total Wimp*. If this is still not to your liking, you are welcome to purchase *The Thrifty Guide to Getting a Refund*, which sells for twice the cost of this book.

I hope all you time travelers enjoy ancient Greece as much as I enjoy cashing your checks. As always, your purchase of this guidebook will support several worthy causes: the Finn Greenquill Vacation Fund, 'cause I want to go on vacation, and the Finn Greenquill Space Yacht Fund, 'cause I want a bigger space yacht. If you're wondering why these causes are important, it's 'cause I deserve them.

Your trustworthy friend,

Finn Greenquill

Finn Greenquill
CEO and Corporate Overlord, Time Corp

TIME CORP LIMITATION OF LIABILITY

By reading this time travel guide, you agree to and accept the following:

1. Cell phone service in ancient Greece is spotty at best. Roaming charges may be expensive. If you don't pay your cell phone bill until you return home, you may find you owe 2,600 years of late fees.

2. King Leonidas of Sparta, general of the deadliest fighting force in history, does not want to take a selfie with you.

3. Aeschylus, the father of theater, totally does. His last play tanked, and he could use the publicity.

4. Plato is the father of modern philosophy. Play-Doh is modeling clay for kids. Confuse the two at your own risk. Anyone who pokes and prods Plato is likely to get slapped.

5. Hippocrates, the father of modern medicine, will not see you without an appointment.

6. Going back in time to kidnap Euclid, the father of geometry, will not get you out of doing geometry homework.

7. Sam Greenquill, the father of Finn Greenquill, does not want Finn staying out past ten o'clock on weeknights.

8. If you discover the lost city of Atlantis, please put it back where you found it.

FINN GREENQUILL'S LUXURY YACHT

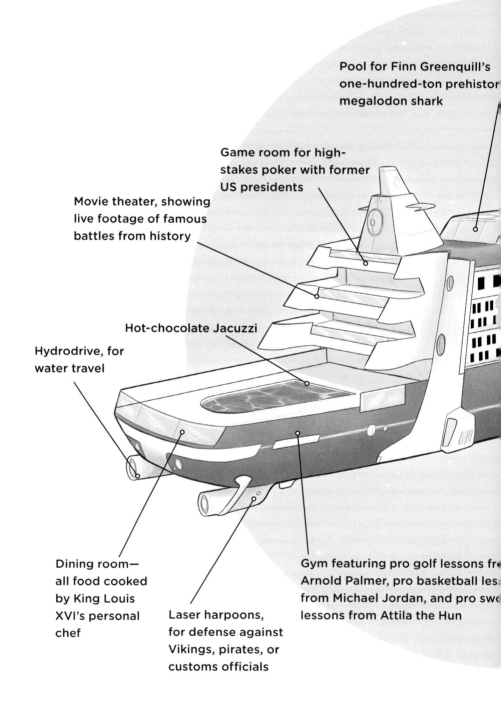

Pool for Finn Greenquill's one-hundred-ton prehistor[ic] megalodon shark

Game room for high-stakes poker with former US presidents

Movie theater, showing live footage of famous battles from history

Hot-chocolate Jacuzzi

Hydrodrive, for water travel

Dining room—all food cooked by King Louis XVI's personal chef

Laser harpoons, for defense against Vikings, pirates, or customs officials

Gym featuring pro golf lessons fr[om] Arnold Palmer, pro basketball les[sons] from Michael Jordan, and pro sw[ord] lessons from Attila the Hun

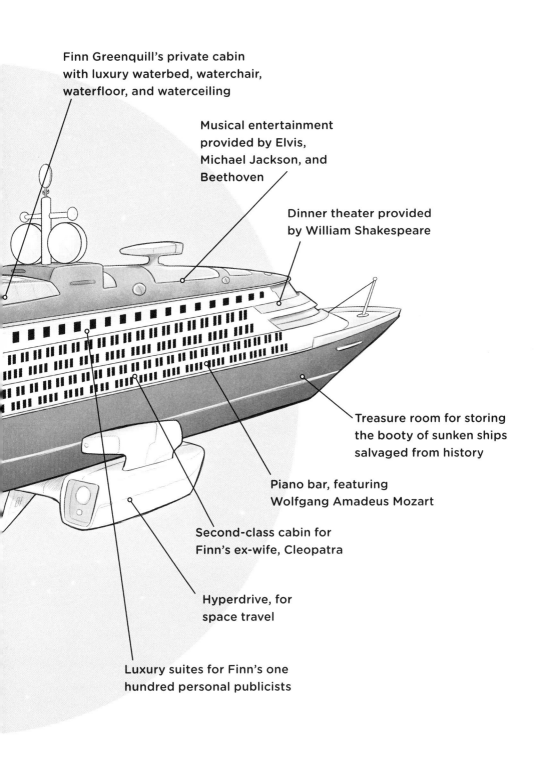

Finn Greenquill's private cabin with luxury waterbed, waterchair, waterfloor, and waterceiling

Musical entertainment provided by Elvis, Michael Jackson, and Beethoven

Dinner theater provided by William Shakespeare

Treasure room for storing the booty of sunken ships salvaged from history

Piano bar, featuring Wolfgang Amadeus Mozart

Second-class cabin for Finn's ex-wife, Cleopatra

Hyperdrive, for space travel

Luxury suites for Finn's one hundred personal publicists

CONTENTS

INTRODUCTION

THE BASICS OF TIME TRAVEL

The good news is, you don't have to be a rocket scientist to understand time travel. The bad news is, you *do* need to be a quantum physicist.

Quantum physics is so mind-bendingly complicated, it will make you want to travel through time just to kick a quantum physicist in the kneecap.

Since quantum physicists make up only .0001 percent of our customer base, we here at Time Corp are just going to stick to the basics. Over the next few pages, we will cover the bare minimum you need to know to time travel . . .

1. Your Time Machine

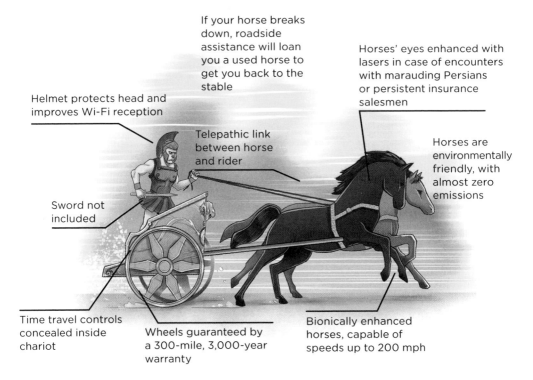

If your horse breaks down, roadside assistance will loan you a used horse to get you back to the stable

Horses' eyes enhanced with lasers in case of encounters with marauding Persians or persistent insurance salesmen

Helmet protects head and improves Wi-Fi reception

Telepathic link between horse and rider

Horses are environmentally friendly, with almost zero emissions

Sword not included

Time travel controls concealed inside chariot

Wheels guaranteed by a 300-mile, 3,000-year warranty

Bionically enhanced horses, capable of speeds up to 200 mph

Who says you can't enjoy style and luxury while blending into ancient Greece? The Time Corp Time Machine Charioteer™ features a glossy all-wood interior, a glossy all-wood exterior, and a stereo to blast heavy metal while you ride into battle. This sporty coupe features an open top and an open back; you may think this leaves you vulnerable to enemy spears and arrows, but just imagine what it will do for your tan.

The Time Machine Charioteer™ is fully equipped with airbags and antilock brakes. Time Corp guarantees this chariot will blend in seamlessly to ancient Greece, though we are not responsible if you try driving this in New York City.*

Please note: Time Corp will retain 50 percent of any money you make from ancient Greek chariot racing.

2. What to Do If Your Time Machine Is Stuck in a Time Loop

1. If your time machine is stuck in a loop, open your *Thrifty Guide to Ancient Greece* to page 3, "What to Do If Your Time Machine Is Stuck in a Time Loop." Read sections 1 and 2.

2. Read section 3.

3. If you still suspect you are stuck in a time loop, refer to section 1 above.

....

* Taking this chariot on the West Side Highway at rush hour will void your warranty.

3. Universal Translators

So your ancient Greek isn't up to snuff. Never fear! All you need is a pair of Time Corp Universal Translators™ (only $9,999 with mail-in rebate!). Simply pop these puppies in your ears, sync the device with your brain, and you will speak and understand ancient Greek!

Side effects may include:

Shrinking hands, fear of sandwiches, enlarged shadow, memory loss and some other stuff, fully functional dog's tail, ear loss, head loss, body loss, loss of reflection in mirrors, ability to hear colors and see sound, ability to talk to fruit, constant soundtrack music, increased ability to smell fear, enjoyment of soft rock, ever-increasing belief that you are the queen of England, in rare cases actually becoming the queen of England.

Troubleshooting: If you have any problems with this translator product, simply call our help line at 1-800-TIMECORP. You will be on hold for roughly the amount of time it will take you to just go ahead and learn ancient Greek.

1
WELCOME TO ATHENS

Congratulations, you've made it to ancient Greece! Any nausea you feel from the time travel will soon wear off, and you won't feel like throwing up again until your time travel bill arrives.

At first glance, you may not think ancient Greece is much to look at, what with the dirt roads, dusty hills, and complete lack of chain stores. So, what's so great about it?

Oh, nothing, really. Only that ancient Greece is the birthplace of *everything*.

The Greeks are pioneers in painting and sculpture. They invent the musical scale. They lay the foundation for the world's architecture.* They even invent theater. Think about that! Before the Greeks, there is no such thing as a comedy or a tragedy.

The Greeks invent democracy, our system of government. They also create the world's first trial by jury.

Hippocrates is the founder of modern medicine—he's the

---

* Finn Greenquill wrote that pun. We, the writers of this travel guide, were adamantly against it.

first doctor to treat disease using a scientific method. Herodotus is the world's first historian. Eratosthenes invents geography. Aristotle figures out that the earth is a round globe. He is also the world's first zoologist, classifying animals into species. Theophrastus is the first botanist in written history. What do these people have in common? *They are all Greek.*

The Greeks are the first people to discover that the earth revolves around the sun. The Greeks invent everything from the waterwheel to the odometer. For better or worse, we have Greeks to thank for geometry and alarm clocks.* Greeks even invent the alphabet that your eyeballs are using to read this sentence.†

So, what's so great about ancient Greece? Only everything. Also, you already asked this question. You may be stuck in a time loop. If so, refer to page 3: "What to Do If Your Time Machine Is Stuck in a Time Loop."

Athens

Assuming your time machine is operating properly, you are now standing in downtown Athens in 480 BC. Athens is the largest city in ancient Greece and home to some of the most important people and events in world history. Let's start exploring.

....

* The philosopher Plato uses a water clock to wake up at dawn so he can get to his school on time.

† The Greek alphabet is considered the world's first "true" alphabet because it gives equal value to both vowels and consonants. It is the grandparent of the modern English alphabet.

MAP OF ATHENS

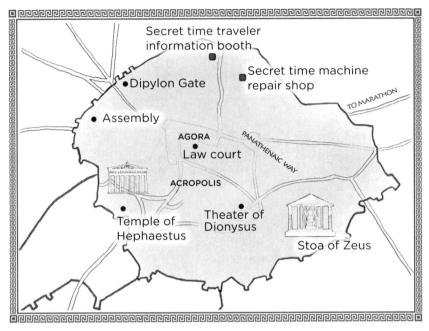

SHOPPING

Why not take a stroll over to the agora for some shopping? You'll find a wide-open arcade packed with merchants hawking ivory jewelry from Ethiopia, linens from Egypt, cumin and coriander from Syria, and dates from Phoenicia. Shopkeepers shout out their daily specials. Fishermen cart in fresh catches from their boats. There are no prices listed, so be ready to haggle.

THE ASSEMBLY

Head up the street to the assembly, the heart of Athenian democracy. Athens is the first place in the world where citizens get to vote for their laws and leaders. *Demokratia* is the Greek word for "power of the people."

Athenian men have the right to vote. Women, slaves, and foreigners do not. One of the things Athenian men can vote for is to ban unpopular people from the city. If six thousand people vote to *ostracize** a citizen, that person must leave Athens for ten years. This, apparently, is how people entertained themselves before reality TV.

THE COURTS

Stopping by the courthouse may not be your idea of fun sightseeing, but keep in mind Athens has the first true courthouses in the world. Centuries earlier, the Athenians elected a man named Draco to create the first written laws in history. It turned out his laws were pretty harsh—according to the Greek philosopher Aristotle, Draco wrote the laws using human blood. Laziness was against the law, and even stealing a cabbage was punishable by death. So the Athenians voted to ostracize Draco. The new Greek laws aren't nearly so harsh, but you still shouldn't steal any cabbages.

FASHION TIPS FOR ANCIENT ATHENS

The key for any time travel disguise is to blend in and look good doing it. Greece is a warm climate, so staying cool is almost as important as looking cool. Follow Time Corp's style guide and no one will suspect you are from the future; they will only suspect you are extremely suave.

....

* For more on ostracism, see the sidebar on page 65.

MEN'S FASHION

Andreas is wearing this lightweight men's linen chiton tunic from our spring collection, and topping it off with a carefree wool chlamys cloak. These muted colors are perfect for blending in with the common people of Athens, who cannot afford expensive clothing dyes, but cannot afford to not look fabulous. Watch out, Athens! On the street, Andreas wears sensible sandals well-suited for the warm Mediterranean climate. In the home, like many Greeks, Andreas goes barefoot. And why not? Athens is a beach city with a laid-back vibe, and you only live once, people.

WOMEN'S FASHION

Sofia will be hitting this year's food markets in style with this ankle-length, sleeveless peplos tunic that says "because I deserve it." Hold on to your chariots! When she goes out, Sofia will accessorize with a veil and a lavender-dyed himation wrap that will be turning heads from the assembly all the way to the agora. Like all fashion-conscious Greek women, Sofia wears her tunic much longer than Andreas; Greek men like to show a bit more leg. Sofia is topping off her outfit today with a fierce combination of gold earrings, silver bracelets, and a seashell necklace.

HAIR DOS AND DON'TS IN ANCIENT ATHENS

One of the biggest problems of time travel—besides all the time paradoxes—is that your hairstyle can be thousands of years out of date. You can try telling the Greeks that your haircut is simply 2,600 years ahead of its time, but Finn Greenquill has tried this in many time periods, and it rarely works. Remember, there's never a second chance to make a first impression.[*]

Here are a few quick and handy hair tips . . .

....

[*] Unless you are a time traveler, in which case there are infinite second chances to make a first impression. But still, you get our point—get a decent haircut.

Men

In 480 BC Greek men tend to wear their hair short and grow large beards. If you visit later in Greek history, the beards go out of style. Stay alert, folks. Fashion is like a shark: if it doesn't keep swimming forward, it dies.

Women

Greek women often grow their hair long, braid it, and put it up. Only slave women rock short hair. Later in Greek history, women will favor tying their hair back or wearing it in a bun. Many Greek women bleach their hair by dipping it in vinegar.

Makeup is popular in ancient Greece. Because rich women can afford to stay indoors all day, pale skin equals high status. So Greek women make their skin lighter by covering it in chalk. Wealthier women use white lead because it lasts longer than chalk, but you should probably not do this, because lead is highly poisonous. Some Greek women are literally dying to look good.

Unibrows are considered high fashion. Yes, you read that right. Sometimes, ancient Greek women who aren't lucky enough to have super-hairy eyebrows will use dark powder like charcoal to connect their two eyebrows together.

For base, Greek women use honey or olive oil to make their faces shiny. They grind charcoal in olive oil to make eye shadow. And they mix iron oxide and ocher clays for lipstick and rouge. If all this sounds like a lot of work, you could always just bring your own makeup kit to ancient Greece.

Places to Eat

The ancient Greeks are known for just about everything except their cooking. The rocky terrain makes agriculture tricky. Beef and pork are simply too expensive. Most ancient Greek meals include bread, wine, olive oil, and not much else.

There are no restaurants in ancient Greece, but at least you'll save yourself some money. There are many taverns (called kapeleia) that serve drinks and snacks, and may even lend you a room for the night. There are also vendors selling hot food in the streets. Try the sausages: they're not too shabby.

Breakfast is eaten at dawn and is nothing to get excited about: just bread dipped in wine. Lunch is also bread dipped in wine, only this time, you get to add some olives, figs, cheese, or dried fish. If you haven't already starved to death, dinner is at sunset. It's usually some vegetables like peas or lentils, some fruit like apples or figs, some fish like anchovies or sardines, and maybe some honey cakes for dessert.

In addition to wine, the Greeks drink a barley gruel called kykeon. If you want to kick the flavor up a notch, you can add grated goat cheese or just salt it with your angry tears.

The Greeks give the world democracy and mathematics, but they will not be giving you a fork. You will mostly be eating with your hands. Bread is both your spoon and your napkin. After you're done wiping your hands on your bread, it's normal to throw the bread on the floor for the dogs or slaves to clean up.

HELPFUL HINTS: SLAVES

Walk the crowded streets of Athens and you may notice that about one-third of the city are slaves. The majority of Athenian citizens own at least one. Slaves do the jobs no one else wants to do, such as cooking, cleaning, farming, mining, and in times of emergency, rowing warships. Bizarrely, most of the Athenian police department is made up of slaves, and—this is true—a good portion of the treasury department.

Pretty much everyone in ancient Greece is one bad afternoon away from becoming a slave. Even Plato, one of the fathers of philosophy, is sold into slavery after offending a Sicilian king. Diogenes, another famous philosopher, is kidnapped by pirates and sold into slavery as well. Aesop, the famous Greek author of Aesop's fables, is born into slavery.

We don't recommend becoming a slave in ancient Greece. We really can't stress this enough. But if you've a mind to try it out, there are a lot of ways to become one. If your parents need money, they might sell you into slavery. Similarly, if your parents abandon you as a baby, which is quite common in ancient Greece, a lucky passerby may pick you up at no cost and raise you as a slave. Kidnapping is also very common when slave traders are low on inventory. Perhaps the most common way to become a slave is for your city to be captured in war. Each time Athens wins a major battle, the agora is flooded with new foreign slaves for sale. If there are too many slaves up for sale, you probably won't fetch a very high price, but try not to take it too personally.

Entertainment

We know what you're thinking. When are we going to get to the Greek entertainment? What about the amazing theater? The epic poetry readings? The art, debate, science, and philosophy? Why are we looking at a bunch of government buildings when we could be experiencing the wonders of Greek singing, music, and dancing? Who writes these time travel guides, a bunch of Greek oar slaves?*

....

* Yes.

First of all, settle down. Finish your bread and olives—you're frightening us. Second of all, we agree. These topics are so important, we've devoted an entire chapter to them.* You'll just have to sit tight. Remember, we're time travelers—we literally have all the time in the world.

HELPFUL HINTS: SCHOOL

While you're vacationing in ancient Athens, school may be the last place you'll want to visit. Still, the Greeks pretty much invent school, just like they invent everything else, so it's interesting to see how the earliest schools run.

First off, you'll need to find out if you're even allowed to go to school. If you're female, tough luck! Girls are educated by their mothers in cooking and cleaning, and don't get to leave the house to go to school.

If you're a slave or a poor person, you can't afford to go to school. Those farm crops aren't going to plant themselves. Stop daydreaming and get back to work!

The only people who get to go to school are rich boys, starting at age seven. They get to learn reading, writing, math, poetry, and music. There are no desks, and school is often held outside under a tree. If you do pop in on a class, pay attention. If you don't learn fast enough, the teacher is allowed to hit you with a stick.

Enjoy!

* Chapter 5.

Religion

Wandering around the city, you're probably tripping over temples at every step. Temples in ancient Greece are like fleas on a mangy dog—they're everywhere. The ancient Greeks are a deeply religious people who can barely cross a street without first making a burnt offering to the Greek god of street crossings.[*]

Greeks often visit temples to consult oracles. Oracles are holy men or women who are believed to have a special ability to read the future. It works like this: say you want to know whether to bet money on your favorite athlete winning a race at the Olympics. Just bring a goat to an oracle. They will sacrifice it for you, and for a small fee, they will cut the goat open and study the intestines for clues to your future. If you think this sounds ridiculous, just imagine how the goat feels about it.

THE ORACLE OF DELPHI

The Oracle of Delphi is the most famous oracle in Greece, and possibly the most powerful woman in the ancient world. Before going to war, kings from distant countries will travel to Delphi to hear her predictions.

A wealthy king named Croesus decides to test the seven most famous oracles in the ancient world to discover who gives the most accurate prophecies. He sends messengers to all seven oracles asking what he is doing at that precise moment. Only the Oracle of Delphi correctly reports that Croesus is cooking a lamb-and-tortoise stew. He is so impressed, he donates a whopping amount of treasure to the oracle and declares her the best in the world.

....
* Hermes.

So how does she do it? The truth is, it may all be an elaborate con. The Temple of Delphi is built over a chasm in the mountainside that spews poisonous volcanic gases. Some believe the priestess inhales the noxious gases; others say she chews on toxic oleander leaves. Either way, she goes into a trance and begins ranting and raving. This is where the real magic begins. The temple priests, who maintain an elaborate spy network across Greece, use their information to "interpret" the priestess's "visions." It is the priests who deliver the prophecies, written in rhymed couplets.

To top it off, the priests charge exorbitant fees for this service—each king must donate treasure to the oracle. The temple is filled with valuables. Some might call these treasures bribes, as a large enough gift can often get you the prophecy you are hoping to hear.

If the priests' spies need more time to gather intelligence, they are rumored to have a trick for stalling. Anyone who wants a prophecy must first sacrifice an animal. Water is dripped on the animal's head. If the animal flinches, the prophecy must be delayed another few days. The rumor is that the priests can make the animal flinch by dripping cold water instead of warm. All in a day's work.

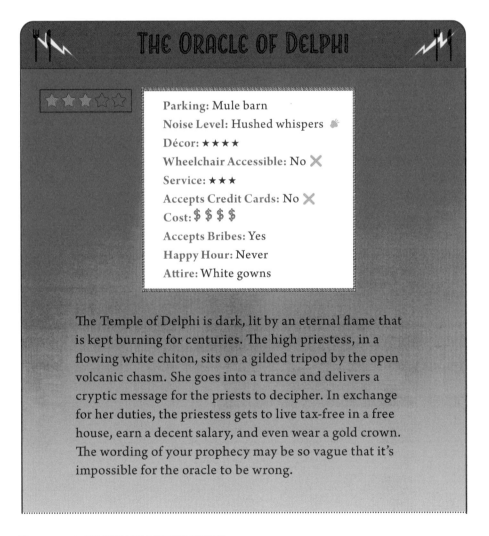

THE ORACLE OF DELPHI

Parking: Mule barn
Noise Level: Hushed whispers
Décor: ★★★★
Wheelchair Accessible: No ✕
Service: ★★★
Accepts Credit Cards: No ✕
Cost: $ $ $ $
Accepts Bribes: Yes
Happy Hour: Never
Attire: White gowns

The Temple of Delphi is dark, lit by an eternal flame that is kept burning for centuries. The high priestess, in a flowing white chiton, sits on a gilded tripod by the open volcanic chasm. She goes into a trance and delivers a cryptic message for the priests to decipher. In exchange for her duties, the priestess gets to live tax-free in a free house, earn a decent salary, and even wear a gold crown. The wording of your prophecy may be so vague that it's impossible for the oracle to be wrong.

Here is what some of our readers say about the Oracle of Delphi:

★ "My prophecy was in ancient Greek. I can't read ancient Greek. It's like Greek to me."

—Timothy L., Weston, CT

★ "I bribed the oracle with three golden chalices and still didn't get the answer I wanted."

—Lucy R., San Jose, CA

★★★★ "The oracle predicted we would get stinking rich off this scheme, and her prophecy was totally right!"

—The priests of Delphi

GODS

Greek culture is filled with more fascinating myths, gods, monsters, and demigods than you can shake a stick at. Not that you should shake a stick at them, but still.

There are twelve major Greek gods and dozens of lesser gods, and generally, they all behave like they're on a sleazy reality show. To help you fit in with the locals in ancient Greece, here's a little info on the most powerful Greek god, Zeus . . .

GET TO KNOW YOUR GREEK GODS
ZEUS

Zeus is the king of the gods, and rules the world from Mount Olympus, the highest mountain in Greece. According to some traditions, Zeus was raised on the island of Crete by a goat named Amalthea. After a war with his father, Zeus became the ruler of the sky, his brother Poseidon became ruler of the water, and their brother Hades became ruler of the dead in the underworld.

Special Powers

Zeus is the god of thunder and lightning. He has a flying horse named Pegasus, who carries his thunderbolts for him. He owns an eagle he trained to fetch his thunderbolts after he throws them. Zeus also has the power to shape-shift into any person or animal, and he can perfectly mimic anyone's voice. This comes in handy when he's sneaking around earth looking for a date.

Relationships

Zeus's first wife is his cousin Metis, the goddess of wisdom and deep thought. But that marriage hits the skids after Zeus eats her whole. Getting back on the dating scene, Zeus sees his cousin Leto for a while, before going ahead and marrying his aunt Themis. She is the goddess of justice and is said to have built the temple for the Oracle of Delphi. This second marriage doesn't take, however, and—running out of family members—Zeus ends up marrying his own sister Hera. She is the goddess of marriage, though oddly enough, her marriage isn't perfect. Hera and Zeus have a bunch of fights about cousin Leto, and Zeus also has a brief fling with his sister Demeter, the goddess of the harvest.*

---

* To be honest, Zeus has flings with zillions of other goddesses and mortals as well. If we listed them all, this would become an extremely long book. And let's face it, Finn Greenquill doesn't pay us by the word.

Staying Alive in Ancient Athens

Athens is just one of many, many city-states in ancient Greece.[*] Each has its own culture. What the cities all share is the same Greek language and a love for fighting one another.

The city-states are constantly at war with each other; it's like a hobby for them. In this time period, Athens is at war three out of every four years.[†] This is important because soon all of Greece will be attacked by the massive Persian Empire, which commands the largest army in ancient history. If the Greek city-states want to have any hope of surviving, they will be forced to work together.

The Persian army is gathering its forces and marching to Greece. But before it arrives, it's time to meet another important Greek city-state: Sparta.

....

[*] They are called "city-states" because they are the size of cities, but like states, they have their own armies and governments.

[†] Wars are suspended every four years so cities can attend the Olympics.

SOME GREEK CITY-STATES

Mount Olympus

Delphi

Thebes

Athens

Mycenae

Olympia

Argos

Sparta

AEGEAN SEA

IONIAN SEA

MEDITERRANEAN SEA

PERSIAN EMPIRE

Rhodes

Crete

2

WELCOME TO SPARTA

War is coming to ancient Greece. And to win wars, you need good soldiers. Luckily, Greece has the best soldiers in the world: the Spartans.

Set foot in Sparta in 480 BC, and here's what you won't find: beautiful art, architecture, theater, poetry, or music. Here's what you will find: the deadliest warriors on the entire planet.

It is against Spartan law for a free man to become a farmer, a merchant, or a craftsman. There is only one job for a Spartan: warrior. The entire Spartan culture is centered around the single goal of training great soldiers for battle.

HOW SPARTAN MEN LIKE TO SPEND THEIR TIME

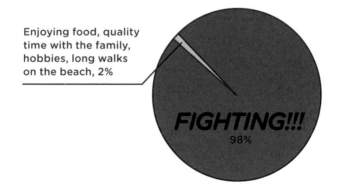

Enjoying food, quality time with the family, hobbies, long walks on the beach, 2%

FIGHTING!!!
98%

Growing Up in Sparta

If you're thinking about settling down in Sparta and maybe rais-ing a family, there's one thing you should know: a Spartan war-rior's training begins at birth.

When a Spartan baby boy is born, he is immediately inspected by the council of elders to see if he is strong enough. If the baby fails the test, he is left to starve to death on a hillside. The ancient historian Plutarch claims the Spartans actually throw their weak babies off the edge of Mount Taygetus.[*]

PRE-SCHOOL

Being a toddler is no excuse to put off your warrior training. Even wee little Spartan tykes are placed on restrictive diets and taught never to cry. Spartan boys are often forced to sleep naked in cold weather, to learn strength and discipline.

OFF TO SCHOOL

If you survive early childhood, at age seven you are taken from your parents and sent to military school. Girls don't get to weasel out of this—they are sent to an all-girls military school to learn wrestling, gymnastics, fighting, and endurance. Spartans believe this will one day make them into strong mothers.

You may think you've had some tough times in your school, or maybe a strict teacher or two. But that's only because you haven't

....
[*] Luckily, Plutarch's claim has never been proven. But Finn Greenquill insists this detail is too amazing not to include in this travel guide.

been through Spartan military school yet. You will have to march without shoes to strengthen your feet. You'll be deprived of food to strengthen your will. Older boys will beat up the younger boys to toughen them up.

This will be your life until you turn twenty. Then you will join the army and live in the military barracks until you are thirty. If you survive that long, you are finally allowed to return to living at home. But your military service will continue until you turn sixty or you drop dead—whichever comes first.

HELPFUL HINTS: THE OLYMPICS

The Olympics take place in the Greek town of Olympia every four years. Heralds around the country announce a truce so that all the Greek city-states can stop fighting wars with one another for a couple of weeks. This allows athletes and spectators to walk to Olympia without fear of being butchered. As soon as the Olympics are over, everyone can go back to fighting each other again.

The Greeks compete in running, long jump, discus throwing, javelin throwing, boxing, and wrestling. They also compete in an ancient Greek martial art called pankration. Pankration is a dangerous combination of wrestling and boxing in which everything is permitted except biting and eye-gouging, and the loser must admit defeat.* The Spartans prefer biting

* The greatest pankration champion is a Greek named Arrhichion. He wins the

and eye-gouging in their pankration, plus they hate admitting it when they lose, and so they usually do not bother to compete in this Olympic event.

In the ancient Greek Olympics, men compete naked and covered in olive oil in front of at least forty-five thousand spectators.* Women are not allowed to watch. There's a law that any women discovered at the Olympics are to be thrown off the cliff of Mount Typaion.†

The only woman ever caught at the Olympics is named Kallipateira. She disguises herself as a male trainer to help her son compete, and her son wins. The Olympic officials decide not to throw her off a cliff because her father, brother, nephews, and sons are all Olympic winners. Instead, the officials make a rule that all future trainers have to attend the Olympics naked.

The first woman to win an Olympic event is a Spartan named Cynisca. While she is not allowed to attend the Olympics, she is allowed to breed and train the horses for chariot races. In this way, Cynisca wins two Olympic victories, and many other Greek women go on to follow in her footsteps.

Olympics three times. He is strangled to death in his final match, but still manages to be declared the winner, because his opponent gives up at the same moment.

* We're not entirely sure why ancient Greek athletes cover themselves with olive oil. Some think it's healthy for the skin, some think it warms up the muscles, some think it smells nice, and some just think it looks good. As for why the Greeks compete naked, that is anybody's guess.

† Throwing people off cliffs seems to be the Spartans' solution for everything. Finn Greenquill is considering implementing a similar policy at Time Corp—it will make the employee handbook much shorter to read.

Spartan Fashion

If you want to blend in on your visit to ancient Sparta, the first thing you will need to do is start hitting the gym. A few days at the tanning salon couldn't hurt, either. Both Spartan men and women do much of their exercising without clothes on, so they have nice even tans. Here are a few style tips to follow, so that nobody suspects you are a time traveler, or worse yet, an Athenian.

WOMEN

While girls can wear their hair long and uncovered, women cut their hair short and wear veils. On a Spartan woman's wedding night, her hair is shaved.

Spartan women wear peplos shawls over very short tunics with slits that bare their thighs. Athenian women consider showing thighs to be a bit scandalous, and refer to Spartan women as those "thigh-showers."

MEN

The Spartan sword is unusually short. Legend has it that when a young Spartan complained to his mother that his sword was too short, she simply replied, "Step closer to the enemy." Another tale is that an Athenian once asked a Spartan if his sword was long enough . . . the Spartan grimly replied, "Long enough to reach your heart."

The Spartan's most valued weapon is his shield. If a Spartan loses his shield in battle, he is disgraced. This is because the Spartans fight shield-to-shield in a defensive wall. If one shield falls, the whole battalion can fall.

Dining Out in Ancient Sparta

We'll just tell you right now: you're not going to like Spartan cooking. The most famous Spartan food is called black broth. It's made of pigs' legs, blood, vinegar, and salt. Legend has it that only a Spartan warrior can stomach it.

The other ancient Greeks despise Spartan food. The Greek author Athenaeus tells us about one Greek who reports, "It's no wonder that Spartans are the bravest men in the world; anyone in their right mind would prefer to die ten thousand times rather than live like this."

In addition to pigs' legs, Spartan men value protein for building muscle. They beef up on hare, goose, dove, lamb, blackbird, and thrush. Spartan boys bulk up on barley bread. You're probably not in danger of putting on too much fat in Sparta. But if, despite the grueling exercise, you do somehow manage to put on extra weight, the Spartans will banish you from the country.

HELPFUL HINTS:
WOMEN IN ANCIENT GREECE

In most of ancient Greece, women spend their lives indoors, running the household. In Sparta, however, women actually enjoy some freedom and power. With Spartan men all living in the army barracks, it is up to the women to take on many of the responsibilities of running the city.

In Sparta, women may go out in public unescorted. This is actually a big deal. In Athens, a woman may not even go to the market without a male escort, unless she is a slave or extremely poor. Athenian women must cover their hair and face with a veil when leaving the house. Married Spartan women must wear veils as well, but only covering their hair.

Spartan women participate in athletic contests, and they may even inherit land. This is because Spartan men are so likely to die in battle. By the fourth century BC, nearly half the land in Sparta is owned by women.

Some women in ancient Greece rise to fame and prominence. One example is Sappho, one of Greece's most popular poets. She lives on the island of Lesbos and runs a school for girls. The great philosopher Plato loves Sappho's poetry so much, he calls her "the tenth Muse" (the first nine Muses are Greek goddesses of the arts). Sappho is so famous, her face appears on Greek coins and on statues throughout the country.

The Helots

So, if Spartans are only allowed to be soldiers, who does all the other jobs? How does their city-state run? The answer is: slaves.

The Spartans rule over a large group of helots, or slaves. These helots do all the farming, all the dirty work, and even most of the clean work. To keep the helots from revolting, the Spartans run a secret service called the Krypteia. Its whole purpose is to hunt helots for blood sport and keep them in a constant state of terror. The icing on the cake is that it also trains young Spartan warriors to kill.

The way the Krypteia works is that young Spartans, armed only with daggers, are let loose in the countryside. If they find a helot who looks particularly strong or fit, they ambush him at night and kill him. Word to the wise: when you time travel in Sparta, make sure you dress as a Spartan and not as a helot.

Spartan Entertainment

Life in Sparta can be a bit tough, so you're probably looking to kick back and relax. Granted, the Spartans don't have much in the way of theater or nightlife. But don't worry, they still know how to have a good time. When the Spartans aren't hunting slaves, banishing chubby people, or throwing weak babies off a cliff, they like to whip young boys.

These ritual beatings, called diamastigosis, are a form of entertainment. Once a year, boys from the military barracks are flogged for an entire day in front of the altar at the Temple of

Artemis Orthia. Not only are the boys expected to tolerate the whipping; they compete to see who can stand the highest number of strokes.

THE SPARTAN BARRACKS

Noise Level: Terrified screams
Service: ★
Wheelchair Accessible: Persons in wheelchairs will be thrown off a cliff.
Cost: Free
Attire: Battle armor

Okay, the Spartan military barracks may not be your idea of a first-class vacation resort. But if you are posing as a Spartan male under age thirty, it's literally illegal for you to sleep anywhere else. Sure, you'll be whipped and forced to eat blood gruel. And yes, you may have to sleep outside, naked, in the winter. And okay, fine, you may have to ambush slaves for homework. But while you can be beaten, these prices cannot! The military barracks are completely free!

Here is what some of our readers say about the Spartan military barracks:

★ "I was forced into a contest to see how long I could stand being beaten."

—George R., Raleigh, NC

★★★★ "I was forced into a contest to see how long I could stand being beaten!!"

—Leo, Spartan youth

GET TO KNOW YOUR GREEK GODS
ATHENA

Athena is the goddess of wisdom and war. The city of Athens is named after her, and in 447 BC, the Athenians build a huge temple called the Parthenon to worship her.

Athena's dad is Zeus. Her mom is Metis, whom, you may remember, Zeus eats. Since Zeus eats her pregnant mother, Athena is not born in the usual way. Rather, Zeus develops a really bad headache and asks his son, the god of sculpture, to split his head open to find out the problem. As soon as Zeus's head is cracked open, Athena springs out, fully grown and dressed for battle.

Among her many accomplishments, Athena invents the flute, though she never actually plays it. Athena also challenges a weaver named Arachne to a weaving contest, and when Athena loses, she turns Arachne into a spider. Athena is Zeus's favorite child, and she is the only god who is allowed to borrow his thunderbolts.

Prepare for War

If you've had your fill of Sparta, you now have this to look forward to: a terrifying war. The Persian Empire is conquering a good chunk of the world, and is now on its way to crush Greece. This will be one of the most important wars in history. If the Persians win, all the Greek advancements in art, science, democracy, and human thought may be lost forever. Luckily, you've had some battle training in the Spartan barracks. And whatever happens in this war, it can't be worse than eating black broth.

Thirty of the Greek city-states meet to decide how to defend the country from the invading Persians. The Spartans are chosen to lead the army, and the Athenians will lead the navy. A spot is chosen for the Spartan army to meet the Persians in battle. It is a battlefield that will now become famous for all time: Thermopylae.

3

THE BATTLE OF THERMOPYLAE

You may be questioning your decision to take a vacation to one of the largest battles in history. Not only is Time Corp charging you an arm and a leg for this vacation package; you may actually lose an arm and a leg.

But we want to make it perfectly clear: this battle won't upset your vacation plans—it *is* your vacation plans. You will have the honor of fighting for a glorious cause. Greece isn't just the most important culture in ancient Europe; it's kinda the *only* culture in ancient Europe. You don't hear anyone talking about the famous playwrights from ancient Gaul, or important scientists from ancient Thrace. You don't hear of any other ancient countries experimenting with democracy or trial by jury. If Greece is defeated in this war, ancient European culture may die with it.

So sharpen up your sword and spear. It's 480 BC and you're about to join the Spartans in their fight against the Persians at the Battle of Thermopylae. Oh, one more small detail, real quick . . .

Only three hundred Spartan soldiers fight in this battle.

How many soldiers fight on the Persian side, you ask?
Five million.

IMPORTANT
Time Corp Insurance Waiver

Hi, folks, Finn Greenquill here. Since you are probably about to die, please sign and initial this insurance waiver before fighting in the Greek-Persian War.

I, _____, being of sound mind and
<small>(print your name)</small>
body, am knowingly joining the Spartan army to fight the Persians even though the Persians will probably kill me. By signing the following, I agree that:

1. Time Corp is *not* responsible if I am filleted by Persian cavalry, skewered by Libyan charioteers, or decapitated by Balkan mercenaries.*

2. If I am swallowed by a black hole during a time travel malfunction, that probably *is* Time Corp's responsibility, but I won't leave a bad online review because I'll have vanished from existence.

3. I acknowledge that the Persian Empire has assembled

....
* Word to the wise: to avoid decapitation, consider purchasing a Time Corp titanium helmet. It's cheaper than head-replacement surgery and a lot more fun!

what is so far the largest army in history, as well as the largest navy in history, and that any Greeks who oppose them are the largest dopes in history.

Pursuant to the foregoing, please initial the following:

_____ I am not a Persian spy looking to gain secrets about the Greek military.

_____ I will not tell the Persian king, Xerxes, about any secret footpaths that may or may not lead over the Trachinian mountains.

_____ I am not a Spartan soldier trying to weasel out of the difficult fighting by pretending to be a time traveler.

_____ In the extremely probable event of my death, I will not get any refund on the unused weeks of my time travel vacation.

_____ I hereby will all my possessions to my dear friend Finn Greenquill.

....
Your signature here

Finn Greenquill

Finn Greenquill
CEO and Corporate Overlord, Time Corp

THE PERSIAN EMPIRE

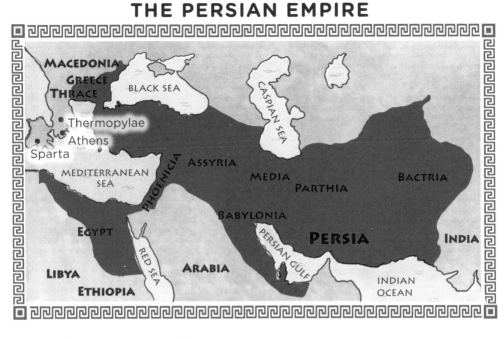

The Persian Army

Xerxes, king of Persia, controls a massive empire sprawling across three continents. But the thing about empires is, you can always make them bigger. Xerxes has fought several skirmishes with the pesky Greeks, and now he wants to capture their entire country. He does not care much about upsetting Greek scientific progress, democracy, philosophy, or the arts—he cares more about conquering people. He marches to Greece at the head of a gargantuan army.

Persia is such a huge empire, Xerxes's army includes the people of fifty nations. The Arab cavalry ride in on camels. The Ethiopian bowmen are clad in lion skins, with their bodies painted half in vermilion and half in chalk. The Libyan spearmen wear decapitated horse heads for helmets, with the ears and manes made to stand upright. But what most astonishes the Spartans are the Persian soldiers who wear—brace yourself for this—pants. The Spartans find this to be hilarious and unmanly.

Xerxes's army is so big, it even includes Greeks. That's because many of the city-states of Greece turn traitor, deciding it's easier to join Xerxes than to fight him. So now Xerxes really just needs to conquer the Spartans, the Athenians, and the few other remaining city-states brave enough to fight.

Marching at the heart of Xerxes's army are the ten thousand "Immortals"—the most elite and heavily armed soldiers in the Persian Empire. They must be in good shape, because in addition to armor, they each carry a shield, spear, sword, sling, quiver, and bow. The Immortals will soon meet the Spartans on the field of battle.

Persian Army Attendance Sheet

241,400 sailors from Phoenicia, Egypt, and even Greece?	**Here**
36,210 marines from Persia, Media, and Scythia?	**Here**
240,000 Persian sailors for transport ships?	**Present**
1,700,000 foot soldiers from forty-seven nations, including Media, Assyria, India, Arabia, Ethiopia, Libya, and Armenia?	**Here**
80,000 horse cavalry from Persia, Media, and India?	**Yo**
20,000 Arab camel troops and Libyan charioteers?	**Check**
24,000 Greek traitors from Thrace?	**Affirmative**
300,000 Balkan foot soldiers betraying their Greek neighbors?	**Here**
2,641,610 support staff, cooks, drovers, baggage handlers, wagon drivers, blacksmiths, and slave-whippers?	**Here**

Total Attendance: 5,283,220*

....

* These numbers are from the Greek historian Herodotus. The Greek poet Simonides estimates Xerxes's army is only four million. Modern historians think both of these ancient Greeks may be exaggerating a bit. But everyone agrees that for 480 BC, Xerxes's army is the largest assembled so far on earth.

PEOPLE TO HAVE LUNCH WITH:
PHEIDIPPIDES THE RUNNER

One reason Xerxes is so dead set on conquering Greece is that ten years earlier, his dad tried it and failed. The Greeks handed the Persians their butts at the Battle of Marathon in 490 BC.

If you can, go back to this battle and try to meet a man named Pheidippides. This poor schlub ran from Marathon to Sparta and back to try to ask the Spartans for help in the fight. That's a distance of 150 miles, and he ran it in two days. Barefoot. After all that, the Spartans refused to join the battle because they had a big religious festival they didn't want to miss.

So, after running 150 miles, Pheidippides fights in the Battle of Marathon. The Greeks win. Now it's Pheidippides's job to tell the Athenians the good news. So he runs 25 miles to downtown Athens, sputters out the words "we win," and dies of exhaustion.

If you have lunch with Pheidippides, do him a favor: try to pick a place that's local so he doesn't have to run too far.

HELPFUL HINTS:
THE MEN'S MARATHON OF THE 1904 OLYMPICS

To commemorate Pheidippides's heroic run from the Battle of Marathon, the 1896 Olympics invented a 25-mile race called a "marathon."* It takes a while for people to get the hang of it. Here are the true results of the 1904 Olympic Marathon, held in St. Louis.

The first runner to cross the finish line is American Fred Lorz. He gives up the race after 9 miles and hitches a ride back to the stadium. But at mile 19, the car breaks down. So Lorz has no choice but to jog the rest of the way. As he enters the stadium, everyone cheers, and Lorz plays along, realizing he's suddenly

* In 1908, the queen of England has the marathon extended to 26.2 miles so her children can watch the race from Windsor Castle, which is 26.2 miles from London's Olympic stadium. From then on, marathon races are 26.2 miles long.

winning the race. He crosses the finish line and is almost awarded the gold medal. When the officials find out he drove half the race, he is banned from the Olympics for life.

Thomas Hicks, also American, is the actual winner of the event, though he should be banned as well. At mile 16, Hicks tries to give up and lie down. So his trainers dose him with rat poison—yes, rat poison—mixed with brandy—yes, brandy. Rat poison in small doses kick-starts the nervous system. His trainers practically carry him across the finish line, which isn't really allowed. Hicks then nearly dies from rat poisoning.

Another American, William Garcia, is also nearly killed. He is found lying in the street by the racecourse and spends several days in the hospital with his life hanging in the balance. His internal injuries are caused by breathing clouds of dust kicked up by the race officials' cars.

Andarín Carvajal, a Cuban mailman, tries to join the marathon but loses all his money in New Orleans. He hitchhikes to St. Louis, going forty hours without eating. He stops in an orchard to eat some apples, which turn out to be rotten. He falls violently ill but still manages to finish in fourth place.

Len Taunyane is one of the first sub-Saharan Africans to compete in the Olympics. He is only visiting St. Louis as part of a traveling circus sideshow. Len somehow enters the race and is a favorite to win until he is chased a mile off course by a pack of aggressive dogs.

Battle of Thermopylae

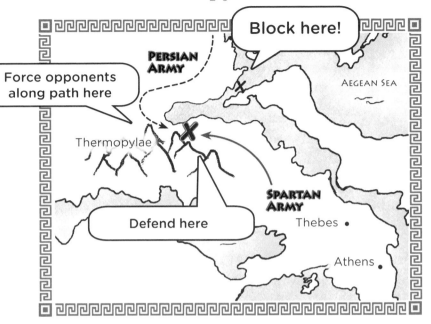

The Persians arrive at Thermopylae in late summer. To invade Greece, their massive army has to squeeze through a tiny pass between the mountains and the sea. It's only just wide enough for two carriages to pass side by side.

The Greeks send their best soldiers to defend the pass: the Spartans. King Leonidas arrives with only three hundred Spartan soldiers to block the pass and stop the Persian invasion. Why so few? The Spartans don't want to miss the Olympics.*

....

* While a lot of soldiers across Greece are attending the Olympics, some Greek soldiers from other city-states do join the Spartan-led forces at Thermopylae. The Spartans dismiss most of them after the second day of battle. Finn Greenquill would like to acknowledge the contributions of other Greeks at the Battle of Thermopylae, but the Spartan tourist board lobbied Time Corp to make this chapter mostly about Spartans.

Here is a helpful chart showing the relative size of the two armies:

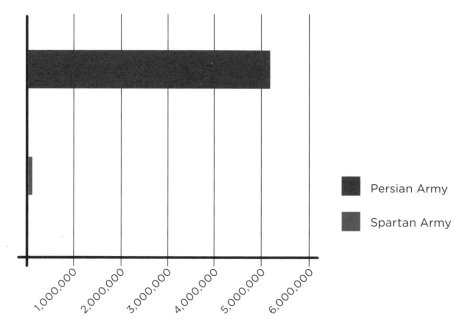

The Spartans know they are a suicide squad. They are only there to slow the Persians down while the rest of Greece prepares for war. Only Spartan men with sons are chosen to fight this battle, so their families can carry on without them. Because Spartan men marry late, most of the Spartans at Thermopylae are over age thirty. King Leonidas is in his fifties. When he leaves for the battle, his wife, Gorgo, asks him what she should do. He replies, "Marry a good man and bear good children." He expects to die on the battlefield, but he knows he is fighting for the freedom of his country.

Top Ten Ways to Help the Greeks Win the Battle of Thermopylae

10. A split second before the battle, replace the Persians' warhorses with saber-toothed tigers.

9. Set up a DJ booth and mellow out the Persian army with smooth jams of the 1970s.

8. Do force fields exist in ancient Greece? They do now!

7. Two words: iridium blasters.

6. Use a Time Corp replicator™ to turn three hundred Spartans into thirty million Spartans.

5. Use a Time Corp Shrink Ray™ to make the Persian army one inch tall.

4. Time jump herds of charging wildebeests into the Persian ranks at key moments in the battle.

3. Replace the Persians' arrows with party streamers, and their swords with toy lightsabers.

2. Distract the Persians with miles of Bubble Wrap.

1. Five million Persians, meet five million and one Time Corp defense lawyers!

The Battlefield

The Spartans block the narrow pass at Thermopylae. Now the only way into Greece is through the Spartan army. The Persians set up camp and wait.

Get comfortable. It's late summer, and the temperature gets as hot as 100 degrees. Rather than charge forward, King Xerxes makes the Spartans wait on the battlefield for four days just to try to psych them out.

Xerxes sends spies to see if the Spartans are scared or planning to run away. The spies report that the Spartans are combing and oiling their long hair and sunbathing. For a Spartan, it's not enough to go to war against five million Persians; you have to look good doing it.

When the Spartans are told that the Persians will fire so many arrows they will blot out the sun, King Leonidas calmly replies, "Then we will fight in the shade."

Xerxes can't believe the Spartans haven't fled the battlefield in fright. He sends an ambassador to King Leonidas, ordering the Spartans to surrender their weapons. Leonidas's famous answer is only two words in Greek: Μολὼν λαβέ. "Come and get them."

HELPFUL HINTS:
LACONIAN LANGUAGE

Even with your handy Time Corp Universal Translator™ earbuds, you may have trouble understanding Spartan language.* Spartans pride themselves on packing a lot of meaning into very few words. This is useful on the battlefield, where a Spartan commander only needs to shout a single word for his regiment to execute a complex maneuver.

* Sparta is in a region of Greece called Laconia, so if you speak like a Spartan, you are being "laconic."

Even in school, Spartan boys don't just study weapons and fighting. They are trained in speaking briefly. Students are punished if they use too many words to answer a question.

This Spartan quality gives rise to some famous quotes. For instance, when Philip II of Macedonia* sends a message to Sparta saying, "If I invade Sparta, you will be destroyed, never to rise again," the Spartans reply with a single word: "If."

When Spartans go off to war, their mothers hand them their shields and say, "With it, or on it." The Spartan mothers are basically telling their poor sons, "Either win or die."

Spartans are so tight-lipped, they don't even write anything on their gravestones. The only exception is if you die in combat. Then your gravestone is allowed two words: "In War."

HELPFUL HINTS:
HITTING THE GYM IN ANCIENT GREECE

Bro, if you're going to war with Spartans, you're probably going to want to hit the gym first and bang out a few reps. There's at least one gym in every city in ancient Greece. Here's a couple of quick tips before you go get yoked.

---

* Father of Alexander the Great. We'll get to him in the next leg of your travel package, in Chapter 6.

First off, "gymnasium" is the Greek word for "naked place." This is because ancient Greeks take off their clothes to work out.

Once your clothes are off, bro, Greek athletes cover themselves in olive oil. After a workout, athletes are usually covered in grass and dirt, since everything sticks to olive oil. No worries, bro. There are slaves to scrape the sweat, oil, and filth off your body. Then—get this—they bottle it and sell it as medicine. Greeks pay good money for the sweat of athletes. They rub it on their own skin to soothe aches and pains.[*]

Bro, if you want to rack up some serious gains, you're going to have to eat the right foods. Milo of Croton is a seriously yoked dude who wins six Olympic wrestling titles. He is said to eat twenty pounds of meat and twenty pounds of bread, and to drink eight quarts of wine each day. He is so strong, he can lift a four-year-old bull over his shoulders. What's his workout regimen? He says he starts lifting the bull when it's a newborn calf, and then lifts it every day until it becomes a bull. Milo is so swole, he saves the life of famous Greek mathematician Pythagoras when the pillar of a dining hall collapses during a banquet. Milo holds up the roof until Pythagoras can escape. Milo wins athletic contests all over Greece until his unfortunate death when he is eaten by wolves.

* We're not sure if it works, but Finn Greenquill will happily sell you some of his own sweat for the attractive price of $9.99 per bottle.

THE BATTLE: DAY ONE

Get ready. It's time for all your training at the Spartan barracks to pay off. Xerxes launches his attack. First he orders five thousand archers to fire a barrage of arrows. This accomplishes exactly nothing against the Spartan shield wall.

Next, Xerxes orders ten thousand of his Median subjects to charge the Spartan line.* The Spartans cut the Medes to ribbons. By relaying fresh troops to the front line, while cycling weary troops to the back, the Spartans never grow tired.

King Xerxes, watching from his portable throne, leaps to his feet in amazement. He is shocked by the Spartans' fighting prowess. Enraged, Xerxes decides enough is enough. It's time to send in his best troops. It's time to send in the Immortals.

The ten thousand Immortals charge. And the Spartans chew them up like paper through a shredder. They trick the Persians with fake retreats, wheeling around to destroy the chaotic rabble chasing them. The best troops in Xerxes's army are humiliated.

HELPFUL HINTS:
TIME CORP DELIVERIES!

How are you enjoying the battle so far? Are you thirsty? Does your sword need sharpening? Maybe you could do with a light snack?

Just remember, Time Corp Deliveries are at your service! Just dial 1-800-THRIFTY and your own personal concierge will pick their way through the front lines of battle to deliver you a refreshing glass of iced tea or maybe a hand towel to mop up blood. Perhaps

* The Medes are from the mountains of northwestern Iran.

your Spartan comrades would appreciate some freshly baked cookies? Do you need any sunscreen? We carry SPF 15, SPF 45, and—for those who want complete sun protection—a hood.

Your wish is our command!

This offer is valid until 480 BC. Taxes, fees, and surcharges may apply. Credit cards will be charged a 25 percent convenience fee. If the delivery person is killed, the cost of their burial will be charged to your account. The delivery person may not be used to deliver you out of the battle. The delivery person will not deliver dire wolves or saber-toothed tigers. This offer expires if you expire in battle. Tipping is optional.

DAY TWO

Xerxes handpicks the most famous and courageous soldiers from every single nation in his army. He throws them against the Spartan line.

They're all slaughtered.

By the end of day two, Xerxes is stumped. But this is when disaster strikes for you and the Spartans. A Greek traitor named Ephialtes[*] enters Xerxes's camp and offers to lead the Persian army over a secret pass through the mountains. He hopes that Xerxes will make him rich.[†]

Under the cloak of darkness, part of Xerxes's army sneaks over the mountain pass to encircle the Spartans.

---

[*] Not a Spartan!

[†] If it makes you feel any better, Xerxes never pays Ephialtes a dime. The only money Ephialtes is worth is the price the Greeks put on his head. It takes ten years for the Greeks to hunt him down, but he is eventually killed by a Greek named Athenades. Athenades offs Ephialtes for completely different reasons, but is still paid a handsome reward.

Letters to Our Complaint Department

Dear Time Corp Customer Service,

I enlisted to fight in the Spartan front lines at Thermopylae. I requested a standard Spartan dory spear, which is up to nine feet long. When I got to the battle, I realized Time Corp actually outfitted me with a Roman pilum spear, which is only six feet long. This put me at a disadvantage against Xerxes's spearmen. I am dictating this letter to my wife, because I cannot type, as I am now in a full body cast. I would like a partial refund on my time travel vacation.

Yours,
Marvin Mullman, Oklahoma City

TIME CORP!™ SERVING YESTERDAY, FOR A BETTER TOMORROW, TODAY.™

Dear Mr. Mullman,

We forwarded your request for a partial refund to our CEO, who was more than partially amused. I have transcribed Finn Greenquill's response as follows:

"Hahahahahahahaha. Oh, oh, God, let me catch my breath here. Ahahahahahaha. Oh my God, I'm in tears. Are you seeing this, Jillian? He wants a refund. I've got tears in my eyes. Ahahahahaha. Somebody get me a Kleenex. Aahahahahahahahaha. Wow, laughter really is the best medicine. Maybe if Mr. Mullman tries it, he'll feel better. Tell him to look in a mirror."

Thank you for being a valued Time Corp customer, and be sure to fill out our online customer satisfaction survey!

Sincerely,

Jillian Mortimer

Assistant to the Second Assistant of the Vice Assistant's Executive Assistant Complaint Department

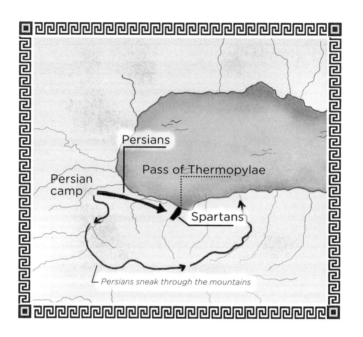

Persians

Persian camp

Pass of Thermopylae

Spartans

Persians sneak through the mountains

DAY THREE

Scouts warn King Leonidas that the Persians have crossed the mountains. This means the Spartans are now surrounded. Leonidas decides to fight to the death. The Greeks have their last meal. Leonidas tells his men, "Eat well, for tonight we will dine in Hades." *

If you want to live, and get the full value out of your Ancient Greek Vacation Package, this might be a good time for you to make a tactful exit. Xerxes starts the morning by launching ten thousand fresh troops at the Spartans. To ensure success, Xerxes has his royal whippers beat his frightened soldiers to keep them moving toward the dreaded Spartan line.†

....

* Hades is the Greek underworld, where souls go when they die. Think of it as a sort of all-expenses-paid Time Corp vacation you can never escape from.

† Finn Greenquill has employed royal whippers to help Time Corp travel writers meet their deadlines, but with mixed results.

The Spartans fight like demons, killing more men than ever. They fight until their spears are shattered, then fight until their swords are broken. Finally, they fight with their hands and their teeth.

Leonidas is shot down by Persian archers. Terrified of fighting Spartans up close, the Persians surround the remaining Greeks and bury them with arrows. When the last Spartan falls, the Persians cut off Leonidas's head and stick it on a pole.

All told, the Persians lose at least twenty thousand men in the three-day fight, including two of Xerxes's half brothers. Their remaining army is demoralized, and quickly running out of food and water. Now the Persian army will march into Greece, and it is up to the Athenians and their allies to try and stop them.

If you visit Thermopylae today, thousands of years after the fight, you will find the battlefield changed. There is a paved highway where the Spartans made their last stand. The marshes have drained and the sea has receded. Centuries of soil now cover the bones of the Spartans, and the Persian arrowheads that felled them. But if you look amongst the fields and olive trees, you will find a simple plaque, written in Greek. It says:

GO TELL THE SPARTANS, PASSERBY, THAT HERE, FAITHFUL TO THEIR LAWS, WE LIE

4

THE BATTLE OF SALAMIS

Okay, stop congratulating yourself. Sure, you fought well at Thermopylae. And if you're still reading this, it means you survived. But the Persians still technically won the battle, plus now they're hopping mad.

The Persian Army Conquers Most of Greece

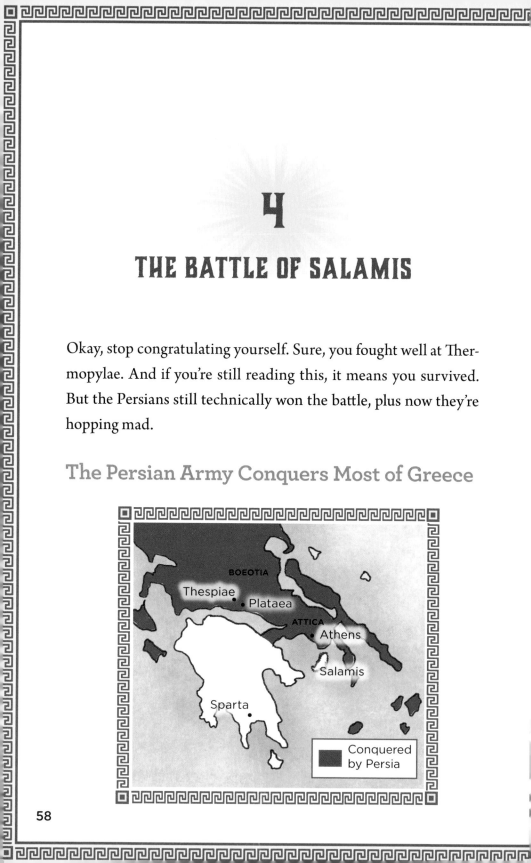

Xerxes's army sweeps into Greece. They conquer the region of Boeotia, sacking the cities of Thespiae and Plataea, and selling the citizens into slavery. They raze villages throughout Attica. The Athenians abandon their city, fleeing to the island of Salamis. The few Athenians who barricade themselves in the heart of the city are slaughtered. Xerxes puts Athens to the torch.

The Athenian navy, with their other Greek allies at Salamis, have nowhere left to run. If the Persian navy can stamp out the Greek resistance, then Greek civilization—and all its gifts to the world—is in danger of being destroyed. What follows is arguably the most important naval battle in history.*

THEMISTOCLES

It's time to meet Themistocles, the undisputed MVP of the Battle of Salamis. Themistocles is an Athenian with a lot of ideas. He helped pick out the battlefield of Thermopylae as the best place to trap the Persians. And he picks Salamis as the best place for the Athenian-led navy to fight the Persian fleet.

It was Themistocles's idea to even build an Athenian navy in the first place. Athenian miners dug up a huge amount of silver a few years back. And rather than divvying up the loot among the Athenian citizens, Themistocles somehow managed to convince everyone to spend the money on beefing up the navy in case of a Persian invasion. The foresighted Athenians built 200 new warships.

---

* Not to be confused with a navel battle. That happens in Mexico City during the Great Lint War of 2162.

All told, Athens, Sparta, and their fellow Greek allies now have 378 ships in their navy. Together, they're going to need to beat 1,207 Persian ships. Themistocles has his work cut out for him. But he has one more idea. . . .

Themistocles decides to trick Xerxes into entering the narrow straits of Salamis. Unable to maneuver, the giant size of Xerxes's navy will become a liability rather than an asset. Themistocles sends a servant to Xerxes, claiming to be on the Persians' side. He tells Xerxes that the Greeks are fighting among themselves, and if Xerxes enters the straits, he will easily win. . . .

Xerxes takes the bait.

WHEN PERSIANS ATTACK

Set your time machine for the Battle of Salamis,* September 480 BC. Xerxes sets his throne up on Mount Aigaleo, overlooking the strait, so he can have a front-row seat to the battle. The Persians sail their warships into the straits in the early dawn. The Greeks sing their battle song. Feel free to learn the words—it's a catchy number:

O sons of the Greeks,

Go free your country!

Free your children, your women, the temples of your fathers' gods,

And the tombs of your ancestors; now is the struggle for all these things!†

....

* Not to be confused with the Battle of Salami. That was in Milan, Italy, during the Great Sausage Rebellions of 2151.

† Okay, fine, it's not *that* catchy. It works better in Greek.

Themistocles has the Greek allies back their ships away as if in fear. This lures the Persians even deeper into the narrow straits. The Persian ships, under the flags of so many different countries, become disorganized and clogged. There are so many Persian ships, they have to sail in three rows, which may become disastrous for the Persians. . . .

HELPFUL HINTS:
YOUR TRIREME AND YOU

Thanks to Themistocles, the Athenians have two hundred brand-new triremes. These ships are fast, maneuverable, and mounted with bronze battering rams to sink enemy ships. The *tri* in *trireme* refers to the three decks of rowers. To outfit your trireme, you'll need:

1. **170 rowers.** These may be slaves, foreigners, or just ordinary poor people. The rowers are divided into three decks. The lowest deck is the wettest. These guys are most likely to drown if your ship is rammed.
2. **20 sailors.** This includes 10 sailors to man the sails, others to steer the ship, and even pipers to lead rowing songs to give the oarsmen a steady rhythm.
3. **10–20 marines.** Athenian ships at the Battle of Salamis carry 14 armored hoplite soldiers[*] and 4 mercenary archers from Scythia.

Battle Plan

1. Speed toward an enemy ship and try to ram them. Athenian ships are more maneuverable than Persian ships.
2. If you miss, your ram may still disable the enemy's ship by shearing the oars off one side. They'll be sailing in circles now.
3. If that doesn't work, your Greek hoplite soldiers can board the enemy ship and fight hand-to-

---

[*] A hoplite is a Greek soldier armed with an eight-foot spear and protected with a sixteen-pound bronze shield and seventy pounds of bronze armor.

hand. Persians wear less armor and have shorter weapons.

4. If that still doesn't work, set fire to your enemy's ship.

5. If all else fails, time jump home. Enjoy a chocolate milkshake, listen to some soothing jazz, and take a refreshing nap. You're too young to die.

The Battle of Salamis

The dawn wind swings in the Greeks' favor, filling the masts of their ships. The Athenians sail into battle. Their rams smash the front line of Persian ships. Like dominoes, the front line of Persian ships is shoved into the second line, which crowds the third line. The Persians become trapped, unable to maneuver their bulky ships in the narrow strait. Many ships are run aground in the shallows and become useless.

A wedge of Greek ships splits the Persian fleet in two. Greek hoplites storm Persian ships and set them on fire. Xerxes loses yet another brother—the admiral of the fleet. He is speared to death and thrown into the sea by a Greek boarding party. This leaves the Persian ships leaderless and even more confused.

Topping it off, many of the Persian sailors can't swim. Xerxes watches the disaster from his throne overlooking the strait. All told, the Persians lose some three hundred ships and forty thousand men.

PEOPLE TO HAVE LUNCH WITH:
ARTEMISIA

Artemisia of Caria is a Greek queen who turns traitor to work for Xerxes.* She's the only adviser who warns Xerxes not to fight at Salamis.

She fights so bravely compared to the Persian commanders in the Battle of Salamis that Xerxes, watching from his throne, exclaims, "My men have become women, and my women, men!"

* Finn Greenquill insists we point out that if you forget Artemisia's name, that's called Artamnesia.

Later Xerxes rewards her with a suit of armor.

In the chaos of the battle, Artemisia does somehow manage to sink one of Xerxes's own ships. But nobody's perfect. It is Artemisia who recognizes Xerxes's brother's body floating among the shipwrecks and delivers it back to Xerxes.

HELPFUL HINTS: OSTRACISM

Themistocles saves the day at the Battle of Salamis, and you'd think the Greeks would be grateful. Instead, Themistocles apparently becomes so insufferably arrogant after the victory that the Athenians vote him out of the city. Remember, at least six thousand Athenians have to vote to ostracize a person. So just imagine how obnoxious Themistocles becomes in order to go from hero to outcast. (This is why we don't suggest having lunch with him.)

It's sort of a common theme for the Athenians to end up ostracizing their greatest heroes. Socrates, the father of philosophy, is ordered to eat poison.* The war hero Xenophon marches thousands of miles

* You're probably noticing the phrase "the father of" a whole lot in this guidebook. This is because the Greeks are the first to do so many things. The Time Corp travel writers aren't sure who started the phrase "the father of." But whoever they are, they are the father of "the father of." And their father is the father of the father of "the father of."

across the Persian Empire only to come home and be ostracized for sticking up for Socrates. The musicologist Damon is ostracized for suggesting that jurors be paid for jury service. Suffice it to say, the ancient Athenians must be a touchy people. You'll do well to smile and be on your best behavior while visiting.

Sadly, official ostracism doesn't exist anymore. But if it did, here is a list of . . .

People Finn Greenquill Would Like to Ostracize:

• People who use "like" more than three times in a sentence
• People who say "a whole nother"
• People who slurp their soup
• People who confuse "their," "they're," and "there"
• People who drive their hyper cars slowly in the fast lane
• Close talkers
• Country-droppers (people who name-drop all the countries they've been to)
• People who clog foot traffic because they don't know to walk on the right side of the sidewalk. Also, all slow walkers.
• People who wait until they get to the restaurant counter before deciding what food to order
• People who borrow a copy of *The Thrifty Guide to Ancient Greece* from a friend instead of buying several hundred copies

Xerxes Is Beaten Like a Persian Carpet

Without a powerful navy to ship in supplies, Xerxes cannot continue to feed his enormous army. So he decides to make like a ballerina and split. Most of his army skedaddles back to Persia, with thousands starving or falling ill along the way.

The next year, the remaining Persians try again. But the Athenians, the Spartans, and their fellow Greek allies destroy most of what's left of the Persian army at the Battle of Plataea. Putting the icing on the cake, the Greeks destroy most of the remaining Persian navy at the Battle of Mycale.[*]

The Spartans and the Athenians learn an important lesson about teamwork and cooperation. Then, after a few years, they say to heck with it. The two city-states go back to fighting each other. This next war lasts nearly thirty years. But that is a story for another time travel vacation.

---

[*] Not to be confused with the Battle of My Kale, fought by militant vegans outside an organic farmers market in Brooklyn in 2025.

5

THE GOLDEN AGE OF GREECE

Time to relax and have some fun. You've earned it. The victory over the Persians ushers in a time of relative peace for the Greeks. Athens, in particular, becomes a hotbed of artistic and scientific breakthroughs. Better enjoy it while it lasts, because more wars are coming down the pike. So hang up your helmet, sheathe your sword, and point your sandals toward Athens; we're going to soak up some Greek culture.

Theater and Nightlife

Head on down to the Theater of Dionysus to catch the latest play. You can see a premiere from some of the most famous playwrights in history, including Sophocles, Euripides, or Aristophanes. The renowned playwright Aeschylus is actually a veteran who fought at Salamis. These guys are

Itinerary

Theater	☑
Architecture	☐
Art	☐
Music	☐
Philosophy	☐

not only inventing theater, they are writing plays that will be performed for thousands of years.

The price of a ticket is two obols (about one day's wages for a poor laborer), but we know a scalper who can score you tickets for one and a half. You shouldn't have too much trouble finding seats, because the theater fits seventeen thousand.

The Greeks are so good at acoustical engineering that everyone in the theater can hear the actors, even without microphones. The seats are called the theatron, which means "seeing place." This is why the entire building becomes known as a "theater." The area where the chorus performs is called the orchestra, which comes from a Greek word meaning "to dance." The part where the actors perform is called the skênê, which eventually becomes our word for "scene."

Greek plays can sometimes last all day, so be sure to bring a snack. Or just use your time machine to fast-forward through the slow parts.

PEOPLE TO HAVE LUNCH WITH:
AESCHYLUS

Aeschylus, the father of Greek theater and inventor of the tragedy, is twenty-six years old when he writes his first play. He clearly enjoys it, because he goes on to write as many as ninety plays.

When he is thirty-five, he fights the Persians at the Battle of Marathon, distinguishing himself in combat. He goes on to serve at the Battle of Salamis, too.

One of his brothers is a hero at Salamis. Another of his brothers is a hero at Marathon, but dies when both of his hands are chopped off.

In the end, it is not a Persian who kills Aeschylus, but a rather large tortoise. According to Roman historians, Aeschylus is killed when a flying eagle mistakes Aeschylus's bald head for a rock suitable for cracking open a tortoise's shell. The eagle drops a tortoise from a great height, assassinating the famous playwright. It's not enough for the inventor of tragedy to be bald; his baldness has to also get him killed by a nearsighted eagle.

Aeschylus's sons Euphorion and Euaeon are also tragic playwrights. Euphorion wins first prize in a 431 BC playwriting competition, beating both Sophocles and Euripides. Aeschylus's nephew, Philocles, is no slouch, either. He writes a play that wins first prize in a theater competition—beating Sophocles's famous *Oedipus Rex*.

If you have lunch with Aeschylus, don't stare at his bald spot. Also, keep a safe distance and watch out for falling tortoises.

Architecture

The Greeks are busy throwing up architectural wonders all over the ancient world. If we wrote about all these monuments, this book would become thicker than most of them. So we'll just mention the most noticeable building in Athens: the Parthenon.

Itinerary

Theater ☑
Architecture ☑
Art ☐
Music ☐
Philosophy ☐

The Greeks use math and symmetry to come up with a geometrically perfect building. The Parthenon, built in 447 BC, is the inspiration for temples and government buildings for thousands of years to come. Look at the White House, the US Capitol Building, the Vatican, or Buckingham Palace, and you will see a resemblance.

The Parthenon stands for thousands of years, despite the best efforts of history's thieves and fools. The Ottoman Turks turn the temple into a mosque in the early 1460s. Then, if you can believe it, they use the building to store gunpowder. On September 26, 1687, the ammunition explodes, severely damaging part of the building and many of its priceless sculptures.[*]

....
[*] If you catch the knuckleheads responsible for this, Finn Greenquill has jobs for them in the building that stores his overdue tax returns.

Art

Greeks are the first artists and sculp-
tors to realistically capture the human form. Take a look at the blocky,
two-dimensional figures of early
Egyptian or Assyrian art—they're
hardly worth the effort it takes Finn
Greenquill to steal them and add

Itinerary

Theater ☑
Architecture ☑
Art ☑
Music ☐
Philosophy ☐

them to his personal collection. Greek art and sculpture is accurate and lifelike.

Phidias is considered the greatest sculptor in ancient Greece. He
designed the forty-foot ivory-and-gold sculpture of Athena inside the
Parthenon.* He also built the massive statue of Zeus in the town where
the Olympics are held. The statue is forty-three feet tall and considered
one of the Seven Wonders of the World.† You can visit Phidias's workshop there and see what he's working on. Most of Phidias's work has
disappeared through history. So if you can smuggle a statue or two out
of his workshop, Finn will make it worth your while.

....

* This statue is lost to history. It is said to contain 2,400 pounds of solid gold, which
is stripped off the statue by the Greek tyrant Lachares in 296 BC. What's left of the
statue is later carted off by Romans, and last reported seen in Constantinople in
the tenth century AD. Finn Greenquill says the statue is absolutely, positively not
in his personal art collection, tucked between the Sphinx's nose and the Venus de
Milo's arms.

† There is some disagreement about what counts as one of the seven wonders of
the world. According to ancient Greek travel writer Antipater of Sidon, the seven
wonders include the Statue of Zeus, the Pyramids of Giza in Egypt, the walls of
Babylon, the Colossus of Rhodes, the Mausoleum of Halicarnassus, the Temple of
Artemis at Ephesus, and the Hanging Gardens of Babylon.* Finn Greenquill says the
eighth wonder of the world is the eighteen-hole golf course he built on the roof of
Time Corp headquarters.

*What kind of maniac puts a footnote inside a footnote? Finn Greenquill, that's who! It just seemed
worth mentioning that the Pyramids of Giza are the only wonder of the world that still exists in
modern times. This is why we charge so much money for time travel vacations—you get to see
some of the greatest sites in the world before they disappear or crumble to ruins.

Music

If the ancient Greeks love anything more than music and dancing, it's math. The mathematician Pythagoras figures out that the reason music sounds pleasant has a lot to do with geometry. He helps develop the scale and chords we use for nearly all modern music.

Pythagoras does this using a musical instrument called a monochord—it's sort of like a guitar with only one string. He discovers he can create different notes by dividing the string into perfect mathematical ratios. Let's say plucking the string produces a note we'll call C. Divide the string in half and you get another C, only one octave higher. Divide the string in thirds and you get a note called G. Divide it in fourths and you get an F. The Western musical scale is based on this.

You can duplicate Pythagoras's monochord experiment using a guitar string, a violin string, or, well, any piece of string. Or you can just go to Pythagoras's house and ask to borrow his monochord.

Philosophy

Philosophy is the study of the meaning of life. Philosophers ask the big questions: is there a God, are we alone in the universe, and why is it impossible to find a decent restaurant open on Mondays?

Itinerary

Theater ☑
Architecture ☑
Art ☑
Music ☑
Philosophy ☑

Pythagoras not only unlocks the secrets of musical harmony; he invents the word *philosophy*. The Greeks produce philosophers like they're going out of style. You can hardly throw a brick in Athens without beaning a great thinker on the forehead.

In Greece, for some reason, philosophers like to spend their time at the gym. There are three main gymnasiums in Athens. Plato's philosopher friends hang out at the Academy, Aristotle's philosophy club chills at the Lyceum, and Antisthenes's cynics are named for the Cynosarges gym. Pythagoras lives in a town called Croton and spends a bunch of time hanging out at the gym with Milo of Croton.

There are many different schools of philosophy. Pyrrho is a skeptic who says no one can know anything for certain, though we're not sure if he knows that for certain. Diogenes is a cynic who doesn't believe money can buy happiness, so he gives up his possessions and lives in a wine barrel. Democritus is an atomist with the crazy notion that the world is made up of tiny building blocks called atoms.

HELPFUL HINTS:
ZENO'S PARADOXES

Zeno is a Stoic, which means he thinks we shouldn't get carried away by emotions. This comes in handy when Zeno is arrested for trying to overthrow a tyrant named Nearchus. Nearchus ties up Zeno and tortures him, hoping to force Zeno to name his fellow conspirators. Zeno refuses to name names, but instead tells Nearchus he has a secret. When Nearchus leans close to listen, Zeno bites his ear. According to Diogenes, "Zeno did not let go until he lost his life and the tyrant lost his ear."

Zeno is famous not only for ear-biting, but also for making up paradoxes. For instance, suppose you want to bang your head against the wall. First, you must move your head halfway to the wall. Then, you must move your head half the remaining distance. And then, half of that remaining distance, and so on. Will your head ever reach the wall?

Finn Greenquill keeps his own list of paradoxes:

1. The more you pay for food at a nice restaurant, the smaller the portion size.

2. The longer you wait on hold with the phone company, the less likely they will answer.

3. And, of course, the Great Soda Bubble Paradox:
   Soda has lots of bubbles.
   The more bubbles you have, the less soda.
   The more soda you have, the more bubbles you have.
   Therefore, the more soda you have, the less soda you have.

GET TO KNOW YOUR GREEK GODS
ARTEMIS

Artemis is the goddess of hunting. Her dad is Zeus and her twin brother is Apollo, the god of music and medicine.

Artemis does not get along particularly well with men, and kills more than her fair share of them. She particularly likes killing hunters. She sends a wild boar to kill a hunter named Adonis after he brags that he's a better shot than her. When a hunter named Actaeon accidentally stumbles on Artemis bathing in a stream, she turns him into a stag and has his own hunting dogs tear him to pieces. Artemis even kills Orion—the one hunter she's actually friends with—when Apollo tricks her into shooting Orion with her bow.

THE TEMPLE OF ARTEMIS

The Greeks build a massive temple in the city of
Ephesus to honor Artemis. The building is considered the greatest of the Seven Wonders of the
World—more impressive than the Statue of Zeus
or the Pyramids of Giza. The Greek poet Antipater
of Sidon visits all the Seven Wonders of the World,
but writes that, "When I saw the sacred house of
Artemis that towers to the clouds, the others were
placed in the shade, for the sun himself has never
looked upon its equal outside Olympus." The temple
is destroyed in 356 BC by a man named Herostratus,
who burns down the temple in order to get famous.
Sure, the Greeks execute him, but he *does* get famous.

6

ALEXANDER THE GREAT

Saddle up your bionically enhanced Time Corp horse.... For the first time in your time travel vacation, we're going to get out of Greece and see the ancient world! Instead of waiting for those pesky Persians to keep invading Greece, it's time to turn the tables and invade Persia ... and maybe a couple dozen other countries, too, while we're at it.

Here in the fourth century BC, most of the world has not even invented the wheel, let alone made the kind of scientific breakthroughs the Greeks have. The Greeks may be able to leverage their technological advancements into building an empire. Along the way, with each country they conquer, they can spread Greek ideas on art, math, music, architecture, and government throughout the ancient world.

But who will lead the Greeks on this campaign across the continents? Who will vanquish thousands of miles of foreign lands? A boy from Macedonia named Alexander.

Meet Alexander

Alexander is born on July 20, 356 BC, in the city of Pella. He's not "the Great" yet; he's just a baby.

His father, Philip II, is the king of Macedonia. His mother, Queen Olympias, is a colorful woman who worships snakes and sleeps with them in her bed. Many ancient Greeks look down on Macedonians and don't consider them true Greeks, because they have slightly different accents and slightly different customs. But once Alexander grows up, we'll see who has the last laugh there.

Education

Alexander is a rebellious kid who burns out every teacher King Philip throws at him. The tutors quit, one by one. At his wit's end, King Philip finally decides to try to hire one of the most famous philosophers in the world: Aristotle.

It's an uncomfortable request because it just so happens that King Philip conquered Aristotle's hometown of Stagira and burned it to the ground. In a word: awkward. Aristotle is easily one of the smartest guys around, and he doesn't come cheap. He only agrees to teach young Alexander if King Philip agrees to re-build Stagira, buy all its former citizens out of slavery, and return them to their homes. Aristotle drives a hard bargain and King Philip agrees. It's just *that* difficult to find a good tutor.

For the next three years, Aristotle teaches Alexander and his schoolmates about medicine, logic, poetry, science, and art. Young Alexander's schoolmates include many of his famous future generals, like Ptolemy and Hephaestion.[*] Aristotle gives Alexander a copy of the ancient epic Greek poem the *Iliad*. Alexander is so inspired by the fabled hero Achilles and all his daring battles and adventures that he models himself after the famous Greek. For the rest of his life, and throughout all his military campaigns, Alexander sleeps with this copy of the *Iliad* under his pillow.[†]

....

[*] Another classmate is Cassander, who will go on to murder Alexander's future wife, but as often happens in time travel, we're getting ahead of ourselves.

[†] Alexander apparently sleeps with his sword under his pillow as well. How he ever gets a good night's sleep is anyone's guess.

HORSES TO HAVE LUNCH WITH:
BUCEPHALUS

Alexander has an undying love for his horse, Bucephalus. The horse is a massive creature with a black coat and a large white star on his brow. Alexander wins the horse in a wager when he is twelve years old. Here's how that goes down:

A horse dealer tries to sell Bucephalus to Alexander's dad, King Philip II. But no one can ride the wild horse, so his father refuses to pay. Alexander announces that he will ride the horse, and he tells his dad, "If I can't ride him, I'll pay for him."

Alexander notices that Bucephalus is shying at the sight of his own shadow. So he calms the horse and leads him facing into the sun, where he will not see any shadow. The horse allows Alexander to mount, and they gallop around the corral. King Philip II is so impressed, he speaks to Alexander with tears in his eyes and says, "Find a kingdom that's big enough for your ambitions. Macedonia is too small for you."

Alexander rides Bucephalus into battle for twenty years. Bucephalus will not allow anyone else to ride him. The fearless warhorse finally drops dead of exhaustion in the Battle of the Hydaspes. Alexander buries the horse with full military honors and names a city in Pakistan after him.

Bucephalus travels thousands of miles in his lifetime, and sees more of the world than most people. If you decide to have lunch with him, bring him some carrots and scratch him behind the ears.

PEOPLE TO HAVE LUNCH WITH:
ARISTOTLE

Aristotle is born in Stagira, Macedonia. His father is a doctor who dies while Aristotle is still quite young. At age seventeen, Aristotle moves south to Athens and enrolls in Plato's philosophy school. He becomes Plato's top student. After becoming Alexander the Great's tutor, Aristotle starts his own philosophy school at the Lyceum in Athens.

Aristotle eventually writes some two hundred books covering topics from physics to biology, from ethics to theater, and from medicine to psychology. His students write down everything they discuss, so the Lyceum quickly becomes one of the most important libraries in the ancient world. Aristotle's love of science rubs off on Alexander the Great. Alexander develops an inquiring mind, collecting animal and plant samples during his conquests and sending them back to Macedonia for research.

Alexander the Great eventually hires Aristotle's nephew to be his personal historian. It's the nephew's job to record all of Alexander's brilliant military successes, basically creating the world's first publicity department. It all goes well for a while, up until Alexander has this nephew beaten, tortured, and killed for refusing to get on his knees and bow down to him.

Aristotle's contributions to the arts and sciences put him head and shoulders above most of the great thinkers of history. The guy is very, very smart. If you have lunch with him, try not to pick your nose.

King of Macedonia

Now almost an adult, Alexander is a little on the short side. He has dark eyes, curly hair, and a ruddy complexion. He spends his teenage years fighting military campaigns for his father, King Philip II, and packing in some solid battlefield experience for the old résumé. His relationship with his dad is a little strained; at one party his father tries to run him through with a sword but misses and falls down because he is too drunk.

When Alexander is nineteen, his father is assassinated by his own bodyguards. Alexander swings into action, desperate to seize power. The army likes Alexander, so they murder any cousins or princes with competing claims to the throne. Alexander sends a coded letter to his mother, Olympias, asking for her help. Like any good mother, she heeds her son's requests, and immediately turns into a homicidal killing machine. She puts down the letter, steps into the next room, and kills Alexander's baby stepsister because she might someday have a claim to the throne. Olympias then convinces the baby's mother to commit suicide. Thanks, Mom!

Alexander quickly races his army around Greece, uniting the feuding city-states under his rule, and massacring the city of Thebes just to set an example. He exiles Demosthenes, the leader of Athens, for talking smack. By age twenty, all of Greece acknowledges Alexander as their true king. For a brief period in history, the city-states actually stop fighting each other.

Now it's time for Alexander to become king of the world.

HELPFUL HINTS:
CHOOSING YOUR EPITHET

Alexander the Great may be good in a fight, but who's got the time machine? You do, that's who. And you know what else you've got? An iridium blaster. If you want to start conquering the ancient world, there's nothing stopping you.

If you do become a world leader, you're going to need a cool name. The Ottoman sultans from Turkey know how to do this; just look at Bayezid the Thunderbolt, Suleiman the Magnificent, or Mustafa the Deranged. These are cool epithets.

In the ancient world, leaders are a little less creative:

Cyrus the Great, Alexander the Great, Darius the Great. . . . You know what they're not great at? Thinking up cool names.

Below are some names to avoid when coming up with your conqueror name. Whichever letter your name begins with, we have an option for you that we do not recommend. From all of us here at Time Corp, you're welcome!

- Abigail the Absolute Worst

- Barry the Bed Wetter

- Christa Who Claims She Has a Boyfriend in Canada

- Danny the Death of the Party

- Elmer Who Eats Glue in Art Class

- Felix the Flatulent

- Gilmer the Gluten-Free

- Heather Who Talks Way Too Much About Horses All the Time

- Ilda the Intolerable

- Jessica Who Only Eats at Jack in the Box

- Kaitlyn the Cousin Kisser

- Leonard the Completely Unfit for Leadership

- Morton the Mouth-Breather

- Nancy the Not Completely Terrible

- Ophelia the Easily Offended

- Peter the Punctual

- Quinn the Quiet Talker

- Roger Who Can't Stop Talking About the Band Radiohead

- Sam the Second Best

- Thad the Thirty-Ninth Best

- Ursula the Utterly Forgettable

- Valerie the Least Likely to Succeed

- Wally the Worst

- Xenobia the Lactose Intolerant

- Yolanda Who Puts Ranch Dressing on Her French Fries

- Zach the Exchange Student

7

GREEK CONQUEST

Okay, so you're probably starting to wonder why they call him Alexander the Great. I mean, all you've seen him do so far is unite Greece and tame an unruly horse. At best, that makes him Alexander the Mildly Impressive.

Well, make sure your armor is strapped on tight, because Alexander is about to go to war with every single country he can find. Take a look at the map on page 91; Alexander is going to march thousands of miles from Greece, nearly all the way to the Indian Ocean. You and he will visit countries no Greek has ever seen or heard of, and you'll go to war with all of them. Along the way, you'll be spreading Greek culture and ideas throughout the ancient world.

WITHIN TEN YEARS, ALL OF THIS WILL BELONG TO ALEXANDER

HELPFUL HINTS:
THE GORDIAN KNOT

In a town called Gordium in central Turkey, there is an oxcart tied to a post with an incredibly complicated knot. Oracles prophesy that whoever can undo the knot will conquer Asia, so in 333 BC, Alexander decides to have a go. Unable to find the ends of the rope, he draws his sword and slashes the rope in two. Ta-da! That night there is a violent thunderstorm in Gordium, which everyone takes to be a sign that the god Zeus is pleased with Alexander's solution, and doesn't at all feel that Alexander simply cheated.

Persia

Greece is sick and tired of being invaded by Persia. It's time to give them a taste of their own medicine, and Alexander is just the guy to do it. His army only has about 40,000 soldiers. Meanwhile, Darius III of Persia has a huge army; ancient sources put the number as high as 600,000. Yet, through his cunning and his horse cavalry, Alexander beats Darius all across the Persian Empire. At the Battle of Issus, ancient sources claim Darius loses 100,000 foot soldiers and 10,000 cavalry while Alexander only loses 1,200 men.* After wiping the floor with Darius's army, Alexander's men finally kill the Persian king. To complete his conquest, Alexander marries Darius's daughter. She isn't too pleased to marry her father's killer, but then again it's so hard to find a good husband these days.

Egypt

Alexander conquers the lands of Syria and Israel, and puts every man in Gaza to the sword. By the time he arrives in Egypt, the Egyptians simply hand him the keys to the kingdom. Alexander's general and childhood friend Ptolemy will eventually get to rule Egypt. Those of you who've traveled to ancient Rome and read

---

* These numbers reported by ancient historians are almost certainly fishy, but nowhere near as fishy as the numbers that get reported in Time Corp's accounting department.

that most extraordinary book, *The Thrifty Guide to Ancient Rome*, have already met Ptolemy's great-great-great-great-great-great-granddaughter. She is Queen Cleopatra VII, who dates Julius Caesar and Mark Antony and rules an empire all the way up until she kills herself with a poisonous snake.

While in Egypt, Alexander builds the capital city of Alexandria.* People from around the ancient world begin meeting here to trade and to exchange ideas. The city becomes a center for learning and culture. Alexander founds the Library of Alexandria, and for three hundred years, it is the most important library in the world.

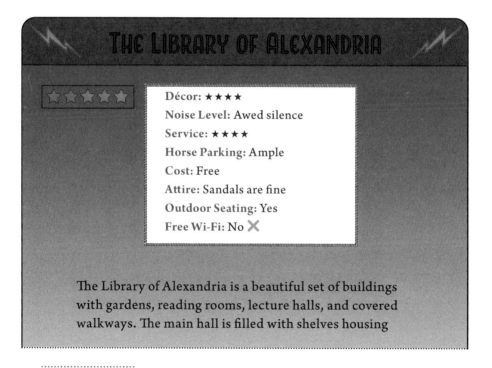

THE LIBRARY OF ALEXANDRIA

Décor: ★★★★
Noise Level: Awed silence
Service: ★★★★
Horse Parking: Ample
Cost: Free
Attire: Sandals are fine
Outdoor Seating: Yes
Free Wi-Fi: No ✗

The Library of Alexandria is a beautiful set of buildings with gardens, reading rooms, lecture halls, and covered walkways. The main hall is filled with shelves housing

---

* According to the Greek biographer Plutarch, Alexander founds seventy cities, and names at least nineteen of them Alexandria. Again, he is not "Great" at naming things.

as many as five hundred thousand papyrus scrolls, with fiction and nonfiction books spanning the whole of human wisdom.

With so many books, the library invents the first card catalog. The head librarians include world-famous scientists. For instance, head librarian Eratosthenes is the first person to correctly calculate the circumference of the earth. He performs this feat without ever leaving Alexandria, using only the sun, geometry, a few measuring slaves, and pluck.

The Library of Alexandria is part of a research institute known as the Musaeum. It contains an art collection and even a zoo. Famous scholars to study at the Musaeum include Euclid, the father of geometry; Hero, the father of mechanics; and Aristarchus, the first person to figure out that the earth and planets revolve around the sun.

Sadly, the library will eventually be burned to the ground and lost to history, so be sure to take lots of pictures. No one is quite sure who the culprit is. One possibility is Julius Caesar, who sets fire to the Egyptian harbor in 48 BC, hoping to burn a few warships, but accidentally burns down a good chunk of the city. It turns out that ancient cities are surprisingly flammable.

Here is what some of our readers say about the Library of Alexandria:

★★ "I showed up in 47 BC and couldn't find anything."
—Sara B., New Canaan, CT

★ "Sorry, my bad."
—Julius C., Rome, Italy

Babylon

Remember the walls of Babylon, one of the Seven Wonders of the World?

The walls are so wide, two four-horse chariots can ride side by side along the top. And the walls are so high, the city has remained unconquered for two thousand years. Well, that's only because those walls haven't yet met Alexander the Great. He sweeps through the entire region of Mesopotamia, including the walled city of Babylon, and by age twenty-five, he is now king of Babylon, king of Greece, king of Persia, and pharaoh of Egypt. But he wants to make one more addition to his résumé: king of India.

India

Porus is a powerful Indian king who stands a foot taller than Alexander and commands a cavalry of war elephants. Alexander decides this is a fair fight. Before the battle, you'll see how Alexander calmly rides Bucephalus through the ranks, giving pep talks to his generals. He knows the names of not only his captains, but even squadron leaders and lowly soldiers like yourself.* He gives encouragement, saying inspiring things like, "Remember: upon the conduct of each depends the fate of all."

....
* What, you didn't think you were just going to roll up from thousands of years in the future and get to be a captain already, did you?

The Macedonians thrust their spears in the air and scream a terrifying war cry as they race into battle. They destroy the Indian army. Despite his war elephants,* Porus loses twenty thousand men, including two of his own sons. However, Alexander is so impressed with Porus's noble conduct, he makes Porus a king of northern India and gives him even more land than Porus had in the first place. After this battle, Alexander rewards his Greek soldiers with a month's vacation.†

Enough Is Enough

Alexander's soldiers schlep 11,250 miles in eight years, to countries they didn't even know existed, and with no end in sight. After the battle with Porus, his men are just done. They've killed as many as 750,000 people and they're bone tired. Three months of monsoon rains pelt them in India. Cobras and pythons slither into their tents. No matter how much they polish their armor and swords, the metal immediately turns green from the rain. They're tired of fighting elephants. And to top it off, after so many battles, there just aren't that many Macedonian soldiers left alive.

So Alexander's soldiers revolt. Alexander's goal was to reach the end of the world. He doesn't know he's only six hundred miles

....

* Anyone who's read *The Thrifty Guide to Ancient Rome*, a remarkably useful and beautifully written book, will remember the Inverse Elephant Law: whichever side uses more elephants loses the battle.

† Finn Greenquill would never allow this.

from the Indian Ocean (which, to an ancient Greek, might as well be the end of the world).* So Alexander decides to lead his men home. At this point in the story, Alexander is thirty years old, and he weeps because he has no more worlds left to conquer.† Don't feel too bad for him—his empire is one of the largest in history: two million square miles, or 8 percent of the habitable surface of the earth.

MAP OF ALEXANDER'S ROUTE

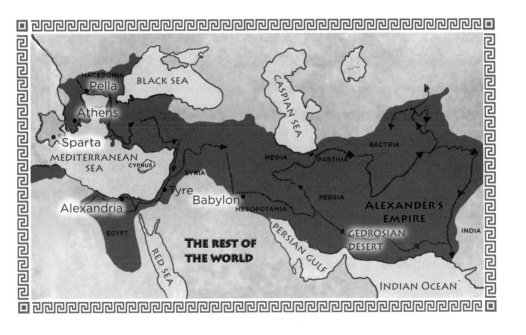

---

* This was thousands of years before world maps, GPS, and Thrifty Guides.

† This was before space travel.

The Long Way Back

Alexander takes a different route home, and so has to fight a whole new batch of tribes.* In one battle, Alexander lays siege to a Mallian castle in India. He is first up the ladder as his men storm the walls. Unfortunately, the ladder collapses under the weight of all the soldiers.

Alexander finds himself on the top of the castle wall with only two of his fellow soldiers to back him up. His men beg him to retreat, to jump back down into their arms. But Alexander the Great does not retreat. Instead, he jumps down into the citadel and kills the Mallian leader himself. For his troubles, he gets shot in the lung with a massive three-inch arrowhead. Does this stop Alexander? No—they don't call him "the Great" for nothing. He keeps fighting until he loses so much blood, he passes out. His two soldiers guard his body until the rest of the army breaks down the castle gates.

....

* Finn Greenquill would like to point out that apparently there *were* worlds left for Alexander to conquer. We're not sure why Finn feels snarky toward Alexander. Probably jealousy.

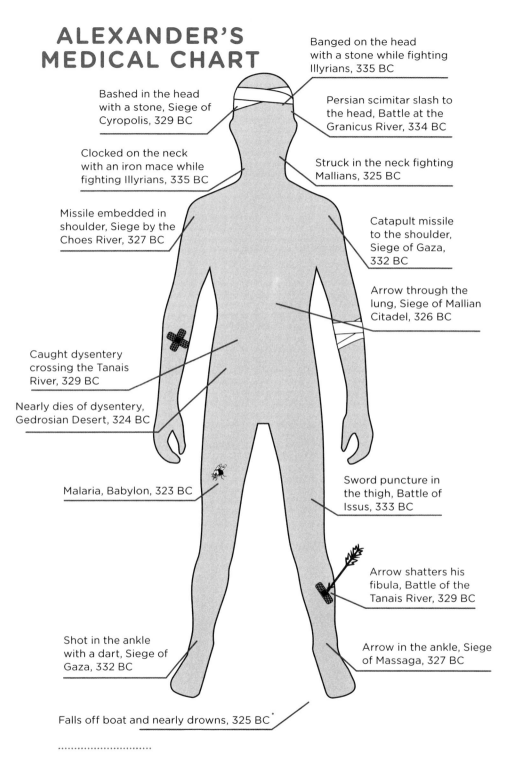

ALEXANDER'S MEDICAL CHART

Banged on the head with a stone while fighting Illyrians, 335 BC

Bashed in the head with a stone, Siege of Cyropolis, 329 BC

Persian scimitar slash to the head, Battle at the Granicus River, 334 BC

Clocked on the neck with an iron mace while fighting Illyrians, 335 BC

Struck in the neck fighting Mallians, 325 BC

Missile embedded in shoulder, Siege by the Choes River, 327 BC

Catapult missile to the shoulder, Siege of Gaza, 332 BC

Arrow through the lung, Siege of Mallian Citadel, 326 BC

Caught dysentery crossing the Tanais River, 329 BC

Nearly dies of dysentery, Gedrosian Desert, 324 BC

Malaria, Babylon, 323 BC

Sword puncture in the thigh, Battle of Issus, 333 BC

Arrow shatters his fibula, Battle of the Tanais River, 329 BC

Shot in the ankle with a dart, Siege of Gaza, 332 BC

Arrow in the ankle, Siege of Massaga, 327 BC

Falls off boat and nearly drowns, 325 BC*

....

* The guy can conquer the world, but he's never had a swimming lesson. Go figure.

HELPFUL HINTS:
TIME TRAVELING FOR FUN AND PROFIT

The ancient world is filled with priceless treasures that will eventually become lost to history. While you're time traveling, think of antiquity as your own personal supermarket. Here is a list of treasures you can go looking for while you're in the past:

1. **The Treasure of Croesus.** Croesus is the wealthiest king in ancient Greece. To get the Oracle of Delphi on his side, he donates a huge amount of treasure to the temple, including solid gold statues, and bowls made of silver and gold. They're stored at the Temple of Delphi if you want to pull off a heist.

2. **Cairo, the City of the Dead.** Here in the fourth century BC, many Egyptian tombs are still relatively new and filled with treasures. Some kings are buried in golden coffins, surrounded by silver chalices and bronze trumpets. King Tut, over in Luxor, is actually buried with several fresh pairs of linen underwear. If you can brave the booby traps, maybe go have a peek inside before the tombs are raided by someone else.*

* Time Corp's lawyers wish to express that we would never endorse grave robbery. If, however, you happen to find anything snazzy for Finn Greenquill's ancient Egyptian collection, he will pay you a pretty decent price.

3. **The Treasure of Priam.** The king of Troy is believed to have hidden away all his silver and gold before Troy was sacked by Achilles and the ancient Greeks. No archaeologist has ever found Priam's treasure. It may be hard work for you to find it, but if you do, you'll never need to work again.

4. **The Lost City of Atlantis.** According to the ancient Greeks, Atlantis is a city that is swallowed up under the Mediterranean Sea. Some scientists think these legends refer to a volcanic eruption that destroyed part of the island of Santorini. No one has yet found the lost city, but if you do, you'll make a fortune selling tickets to time travel tourists.

5. **The Mallian Tribute.** After Alexander the Great defeats the Mallians in India, they pay him off with a tribute of 300 four-horse chariots, 1,000 Indian shields, a number of lions, and 100 talents of silver (5,732 pounds, or nearly two million dollars). If you can intercept this delivery with, say, a few iridium blasters and a time machine, it will be a profitable afternoon's work.

Return to Babylon

Alexander's army crosses the Gedrosian Desert, trying to get home. They travel fifty miles without water until they finally reach some brackish mud. Men jump in with full armor and drink too much water too quickly and die. Others try eating a species of cucumber they find, but the cucumbers explode, blinding and poisoning the men.* Other soldiers die of heatstroke. Finally, a flash flood strikes, killing many of the soldiers and all their wives and children. Alexander enters the desert with eighty-five thousand people and leaves with twenty-five thousand. By the time his soldiers crawl out of the desert, they have nothing but their weapons and the clothes on their backs.

Letters to Our Complaint Department

Dear Time Corp Customer Service,

I enlisted in Alexander's army. Your brochure made it sound like a blast. "See the world!" "Improve your tan!" "Enjoy a great cardio workout while on a paleo diet!"

11,250 miles. That's how far I've walked. In sandals. You know what I can tell you about sandals? No arch support! And you know what else? Blisters. I want to walk right into Time Corp and tell you exactly what I think, but I would only get more blisters. And I can't leave the army, or

....

* *Ecballium elaterium*, otherwise known as "the exploding cucumber," is a real species. If you try to eat it, you're going to have a bad time.

Alexander the Great will hang me for desertion.

Thanks a lot, Time Corp!

Keven Sulkmeier, Oconomowoc, WI

TIME CORP! ™ **SERVING YESTERDAY, FOR A BETTER TOMORROW, TODAY.** ™

Dear Mr. Sulkmeier,

You're welcome!

Sincerely,

Jillian Mortimer

Assistant to the Second Assistant of the

Vice Assistant's Executive Assistant

Complaint Department

Alexander the Great Drunk

Alexander is said to exceed all men in his drinking. He considers beer to be a peasant drink and prefers to drink a strong wine that is about 10 percent alcohol. Once he arrives in Babylon, he decides to stay there for a bit because it is closer to the center of his empire. There are many days when he does nothing but drink. Like his father, he often gets into drunken brawls. In one brawl, he stabs his friend Cleitus the Black to death, even though Cleitus saved Alexander's life at the Battle of Granicus River. If Alexander does invite you out for a night on the town, just keep an eye on him and make sure he doesn't stab you.

Death of Alexander

Alexander's drinking ultimately leads to his downfall. While suffering from a fever, he decides to go out drinking with his friends instead of staying home in bed. Just when he's starting to really feel bad, one of his buddies invites him to yet another party. Alexander stays out all night. By the morning, he is in truly bad shape. The last two weeks of his life are spent in a high fever. He dies in Babylon on June 13, 323 BC, at age thirty-two.

With Alexander gone, his empire quickly collapses. His generals carve up the territory, battling each other for land. The influence of Greek culture across the ancient world begins a steady decline. The lesson is this: if you're feeling under the weather, maybe stay home and drink some chicken soup.

PEOPLE TO HAVE LUNCH WITH: ROXANA

Roxana is one of Alexander's three wives, and is considered one of the most beautiful women in the world. She is a Persian princess of Bactria. She and Alexander meet in the usual way: he's besieging her father in a mountain fortress; she's running for her life. He's twenty-nine; she's thirteen. Finn Greenquill's parents met in more or less the same way. Suffice it to say, Alexander sees Roxana and falls in love at first sight.

Alexander marries Roxana despite the objections of his friends and generals. As a wedding present, he stops trying to kill her father and instead makes him the governor of Punjab, India.

By all accounts, Alexander and Roxana get along pretty well. Granted, it's not a traditional marriage. Alexander's boyfriend is best man at the wedding. Plus, Alexander has two other wives, as well as over 365 concubines* he keeps in Babylon (one for every day of the year, as is the tradition for Babylonian rulers). Still, Roxana is Alexander's favorite wife, and in a romantic gesture, he even promotes her brother to his elite cavalry division.

A few months after Alexander dies, seventeen-year-old Roxana gives birth to his only son. Even though Alexander left no other children, Roxana isn't taking any chances. She murders his two other wives, and even some of their family members. You really can't be too careful when it comes to inheritances.

Roxana goes to live with Alexander's mother, Olympias, in Macedonia. They have a lot in common, since Olympias also killed a bunch of family members. Unfortunately, one of Alexander's old school chums, Cassander, takes over Greece and assassinates Olympias, Roxana, and Alexander's son.

If you have lunch with Roxana, try to stay on her good side. And whatever you do, don't let Alexander catch you at a fancy restaurant with his wife—he may take it the wrong way.

---

* A concubine is like a wife whose birthday you never need to remember. Concubines have lower status than wives, and their kids usually cannot inherit the throne. Being a concubine is a pretty thankless job, but it beats working for Time Corp Customer Service.

8

THE FALL OF THE GREEK EMPIRE

Sorry, ancient Greece. There's a new player in town: the Roman Empire. Alexander the Great was planning on conquering these Roman upstarts, but fever conquered him first. As Rome grows, it begins to threaten its Greek neighbors, and the Greeks are nervous.

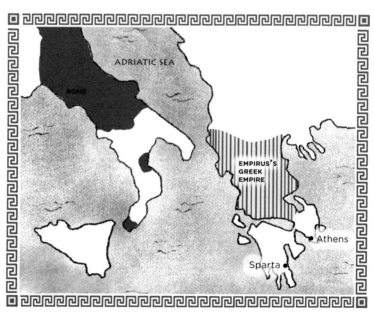

In 280 BC, the Greek general Pyrrhus of Epirus decides it's time to show the Romans who's boss. Pyrrhus sails to Italy with 20,000 foot soldiers, 3,000 cavalry, 2,000 archers, 500 slingers, and 20 war elephants. He beats the Roman army at the Battle of Heraclea and again at the Battle of Asculum, but at enormous cost. Most of his best soldiers are slaughtered. After the Battle of Asculum, Pyrrhus famously says, "If we are victorious in one more battle with the Romans, we shall be utterly ruined."[*] Pyrrhus gives up fighting Romans and instead takes a job as the king of Sicily.

PEOPLE TO HAVE LUNCH WITH:
CHRYSIPPUS

Chrysippus is a Greek philosopher who lives in Athens about seventy-five years after the death of Alexander the Great. He'll be delighted to have lunch with you, particularly if you pay—he is once quoted as saying that the best meal is a free one.

In addition to his hobby of long-distance running, Chrysippus runs Zeno's school of Stoic philosophy. Stoics believe in controlling emotions and leading a virtuous life. Chrysippus creates at least 500 lines of writing per day, and produces over 705 written works.[†]

[*] This is the origin of the term "pyrrhic victory," which means to win at devastating cost. Time Corp's legal department tries to explain this concept to Finn Greenquill before each of his legal escapades, but he never seems to really get it.

[†] This amazing amount of work puts Time Corp's travel writers to shame. Finn Greenquill offered big bucks trying to hire Chrysippus, but the philosopher told him that money doesn't buy happiness. Shows what he knows.

> In 206 BC, the great Stoic philosopher literally dies of laugher. Apparently, Chrysippus is watching a donkey eating some figs when he suddenly cries out, "Now give the donkey a drink of pure wine to wash down those figs!" He bursts into hysterics, laughing at his own bizarre joke. He laughs so hard, he has either a brain aneurism or a heart attack. He keels over and dies. All in all, there are worse ways to go.

The Romans Grow Stronger

In 200 BC, the Romans score their first major military victory over Greece in a series of battles called the Second Macedonian War. Within three years, the Macedonian king Philip V loses all of southern Greece, Bulgaria, and Turkey to the Roman forces. In 86 BC, the Roman general Sulla captures Athens. Greece is now a subject of the Roman Empire, and many Greeks are sold into slavery.

Nevertheless, Greek culture continues to pump out an astonishing number of great thinkers, such as Aedesia, one of the first female philosophers; Euclid, the father of geometry;[*] and Hipparchus, the father of trigonometry.[†]

....

[*] Time Corp's travel writers would like to apologize for calling Euclid "the father of geometry" three separate times in this book. We're sure he has other fine qualities. The thing is, we really can't overstate how important Euclid is to geometry. His math textbook *Elements* is one of the most influential books in history. Over one thousand editions have been printed over the centuries, making *Elements* second only to the Bible in continued popularity.

[†] Thanks a lot, Hipparchus.

PEOPLE TO HAVE LUNCH WITH:
ARCHIMEDES

Archimedes is a Greek scientist and inventor who lives in Italy about fifty years after the death of Alexander the Great. He studies math at Euclid's school in Alexandria. He is considered one of the greatest mathematicians of all time, discovering how to calculate the area and volume of spheres, and more accurately measure circles and cones.

When his hometown is attacked by the Roman navy, Archimedes defends his city with incredible inventions. He designs a machine called the Claw of Archimedes that destroys enemy ships by lifting them out of the water.

He invents powerful siege weapons and a screw pump for moving water uphill. He builds catapults to hurl giant stones. And he even invents a heat ray, using a complex system of mirrors to set enemy ships on fire.* While it is unclear how well this invention works, it's worth pointing out that Roman ships are covered in tar to seal the wood from leaks, making the ships super flammable.

Archimedes discovers the principles of fluid dynamics when the Greek Sicilian king Hieron of Syracuse approaches him with a problem. The king suspects his crown maker cheated him by using silver in a crown that is supposed to be pure gold. The king wants Archimedes to figure out if the crown is pure.

The problem utterly stumps Archimedes. Finally

---

* Finn Greenquill would *kill* for one of these. He's never wanted anything so badly. Except for that giant squid catapult he overpaid for. And that mind-reading helmet that broke when he accidentally ran it through the washing machine.

one day, stepping into his bath, he sees the relationship between his body's mass and the amount of water overflowing his tub. Overwhelmed, he runs through the streets naked, yelling "Eureka!" (Greek for "I've found it!"). Archimedes compares the displacements of silver and gold in water, and proves that the king was cheated.

Archimedes leads a long life, but he is ultimately killed while doing his homework. When the Romans finally conquer Syracuse in 212 BC, they're under instructions not to harm the seventy-five-year-old inventor, because they want him to build war machines for Rome. A soldier bursts into Archimedes's home and demands the great thinker report immediately to the Roman general. Archimedes is so intent on his studies that he refuses to leave his calculations. The soldier gets angry and begins stomping on Archimedes's geometry drawings. Archimedes's last words are, "Don't disturb my circles!" The soldier stabs Archimedes to death.

For all of Archimedes's work on exponents, pulleys, levers, and geometry, he considers his proof of the area of a sphere to be his most important idea. And he leaves instructions for the proof to be written on his gravestone.*

....

* The famous Roman lawyer Cicero actually finds Archimedes's tomb in 75 BC, but it has since been lost to history. If you can track it down, Time Corp will pay you big bucks! Or at least medium bucks.

The Goths and the Slavs

You know the party's over when the Goths show up. They sweep down through Poland and across Central Europe. In 267 AD, the Goths sack Athens, Sparta, and Corinth. In 641 AD, the Slavs—a tribe invading from Central Europe—overrun Greece, destroying anything the Goths missed. That's pretty much it. Greece is conquered and its people scattered.

Yet in a way, ancient Greece never truly dies. It lives on in modern cultures across the world. Wherever there is democracy, from Norway to New Zealand, Greek culture lives on. Wherever modern medicine is practiced as a science, Greek culture lives on. (Perhaps as much as 75 percent of medical terminology is still expressed in Greek.) Wherever tragedies or comedies are performed on a stage, or wherever a piece of music uses a major or minor scale, we have the Greeks to thank. And for those of us who think the earth revolves around the sun, or that the world is composed of atoms, we must tip our hats to the Greeks as well. Ancient Greece is all around us. And this is the strange beauty of time travel. By visiting the past, we learn about our present.

From all of us here at Time Corp, thank you for traveling with us, and thanks for all the money!

TIME CORP! ™ SERVING YESTERDAY, FOR A BETTER TOMORROW, TODAY.™

A FRIENDLY MESSAGE FROM YOUR CORPORATE OVERLORD AT TIME CORP,
FINN GREENQUILL

If you're still reading, it means you managed to survive ancient Greece. This is probably good news for you, but it's absolutely great news for me, as it means you won't be cashing in your Time Corp life insurance policy.

There are people who say I only sell travel packages to incredibly dangerous periods in history so I can profit off selling more Time Corp life insurance policies. This is an outright lie! And I'm a guy who can spot a lie because I lie constantly. I've already lied four times in this paragraph. Or have I? Who knows! The point is, some people pay so much for Time Corp life insurance policies that they're disappointed when they actually come back alive.

On behalf of all the valuable employees here at Time Corp (namely me), I would like to thank you for time traveling with us. We realize there are a lot of other time

CHAPTER 8: THE FALL OF THE GREEK EMPIRE 113

travel companies you could have chosen, if I hadn't bought them all and run them into bankruptcy.

If you somehow survived the Battle of Thermopylae and the Battle of Salamis, you may have a few less limbs than you started out with. But look on the bright side, at least you've lost weight. And as long as you still have enough fingers to hold a credit card, you can continue to spend your remaining money on more time travel vacations.

Wealthily,

Finn Greenquill

Finn Greenquill
CEO and Corporate Overlord, Time Corp

SELECTED BIBLIOGRAPHY

Arrian. *Anabasis of Alexander.* Translated by P. A. Brunt. Cambridge: Harvard University Press, 1976.

Cantor, Norman F. *Alexander the Great: Journey to the End of the Earth.* New York: HarperCollins, 2005.

Cartledge, Paul. *Thermopylae: The Battle That Changed the World.* New York: The Overlook Press, 2006.

Herodotus. *The Histories.* Translated by Aubrey De Sélincourt. Edited with an introduction by John Marincola. New York: Penguin Classics, 2003.

Plutarch. *Plutarch on Sparta.* Translated, edited, and with an introduction by Richard J. A. Talbert. New York: Penguin Classics, 1988.

Savill, Agnes. *Alexander the Great and His Time.* New York: Marboro Books, 1990.

ACKNOWLEDGMENTS

The travel writers at Time Corp would like to thank Xerxes, Darius III, Alexander the Great, Finn Greenquill, and all the other despotic rulers who threatened to kill us during the writing of this book, but ultimately didn't.

A special thanks to Leila Sales, who not only works for Penguin, but her name is an anagram for "Seal Allies." Coincidence? You decide.

A grateful tip of the hat to copyeditor Janet Pascal, whose name is an anagram for "a pal can jest." A heartfelt merci beaucoup to fact-checker Lawrence Bliquez, who belongs to a "New Blazer Clique." A humble muchas gracias to copyeditor Laura Stiers, who is actually "a surrealist." A big thank-you to art director Jim Hoover, whose name is almost impossible to anagram, though "James Hoover" gets you "save her mojo." And a grateful bow to junior designer Mariam Quraishi, who doesn't seem particularly dangerous, even though her name spells "I harm Samurai Qi."

Jonathan W. Stokes is a former teacher turned Hollywood screenwriter, who has written screenplays for Warner Brothers, Universal, Fox, Paramount, New Line, and Sony/Columbia. Inspired by a childhood love of *The Goonies* and *Ferris Bueller's Day Off*, Jonathan writes the Addison Cooke series as well as the other books in the Thrifty Guide series. Raised in Connecticut, he currently resides in Los Angeles, where he can be found showing off his incredible taste in dishware and impressive 96 percent accuracy with high fives.

Xavier Bonet is an illustrator and a comic book artist who lives in Barcelona with his wife and two children. He has illustrated a number of middle grade books including *Omnia* by Laura Gallego, Michael Dahl's Really Scary Stories series, and the Keepers trilogy by Lian Tanner. He loves all things retro, video games, and Japanese food, but above all, spending time with his family. Visit him at xavierbonet.net and follow him on Twitter or Instagram @xbonetp.

YOUR ADVENTURES ARE JUST BEGINNING!

Wherever you go on your next vacation,
be sure to bring along a Thrifty Guide to
get the most out of your trip.

Coming soon:

THE THRIFTY GUIDE TO
MEDIEVAL TIMES